Amazon Comprehend Developer Guide

A catalogue record for this book is available from the Hong Kong Public Libraries.

Published in Hong Kong by Samurai Media Limited.

Email: info@samuraimedia.org

ISBN 9789888408351

Contents

What Is Amazon Comprehend?   **5**
    Topic Modelling 5
    Examples 5
    Benefits 6
    Are You a First-time User of Amazon Comprehend? 6

How It Works   **7**

Detecting Entities   **8**

Detecting Key Phrases   **9**
    Detecting Key Phrases Using the AWS Command Line Interface 9
    Detecting Key Phrases Using the AWS SDK for Java 9
    Detecting Key Phrases Using the AWS SDK for Python (Boto) 10

Detecting the Primary Language   **11**

Detecting Sentiments   **12**

Batch Processing Documents   **14**

Topic Modeling   **17**
    Before You Start 17
    Topic Modeling Using the AWS Command Line Interface 17
    Topic Modeling Using the AWS SDK for Java 19
    Topic Modeling Using the AWS SDK for Python (Boto) 20

Getting Started with Amazon Comprehend   **22**

Step 1: Set Up an AWS Account and Create an Administrator User   **23**
    Sign Up for AWS 23
    Create an IAM User 23
    Next Step 24

Step 2: Set Up the AWS Command Line Interface (AWS CLI)   **25**
    Next Step 25

Step 3: Getting Started Using the Amazon Comprehend Console   **26**

Analyzing Documents Using the Console   **27**

Creating a Topic Modeling Job Using the Console   **31**

Step 4: Getting Started Using the Amazon Comprehend API   **34**

Detecting the Dominant Language   **35**
    Detecting the Dominant Language Using the AWS Command Line Interface 35
    Detecting the Dominant Language Using the AWS SDK for Java 35
    Detecting the Dominant Language Using the AWS SDK for Python (Boto) 36

Detecting Named Entities   **37**
    Detecting Named Entities Using the AWS Command Line Interface 37
    Detecting Named Entities Using the AWS SDK for Java 37
    Detecting Named Entities Using the AWS SDK for Python (Boto) 38

Detecting Sentiment **39**

    Detecting Sentiment Using the AWS Command Line Interface 39

    Detecting Sentiment Using the AWS SDK for Java 39

    Detecting Sentiment Using the AWS SDK for Python (Boto) 40

Using the Batch APIs **41**

    Batch Processing With the SDK for Java 41

What Is Amazon Comprehend?

Amazon Comprehend uses natural language processing (NLP) to extract insights about the content of documents. Amazon Comprehend processes any text file in UTF-8 format. It develops insights by recognizing the entities, key phrases, language, sentiments, and other common elements in a document. Use Amazon Comprehend to create new products based on understanding the structure of documents. For example, using Amazon Comprehend you can search social networking feeds for mentions of products or scan an entire document repository for key phrases.

You work with one document at a time to detect entities, key phrases, languages, and sentiments. Each document is processed separately. Some of the insights that Amazon Comprehend develops about a document include:

- **Entities** – Amazon Comprehend returns a list of entities, such as people, places, and locations, identified in a document. For more information, see Detecting Entities.

- **Key phrases** – Amazon Comprehend extracts key phrases that appear in a document. For example, a document about a basketball game might return the names of the teams, the name of the venue, and the final score. For more information, see Detecting Key Phrases.

- **Language** – Amazon Comprehend identifies the dominant language in a document. Amazon Comprehend can identify 100 languages. For more information, see Detecting the Primary Language .

- **Sentiment** – Amazon Comprehend determines the emotional sentiment of a document. Sentiment can be positive, neutral, negative, or mixed. For more information, see Detecting Sentiments.

Topic Modelling

You can also use Amazon Comprehend to examine a corpus of documents to find the common themes contained within the corpus. Amazon Comprehend examines the documents in the corpus and then returns the most prominent topics and the documents that are associated with each topic.

Topic modeling is a asynchronous process, you submit a set of documents for processing and then later get the results when processing is complete. Amazon Comprehend does topic modeling on large document sets, for best results you should include at least 1,000 documents when you submit a topic modeling job. For more information, see Topic Modeling.

Examples

The following examples show how you might use the Amazon Comprehend operations in your applications.

Example 1: Find documents about a subject
Find the documents about a particular subject using Amazon Comprehend topic modeling. Scan a set of documents to determine the topics discussed, and to find the documents associated with each topic. You can specify the number of topics that Amazon Comprehend should return from the document set.

Example 2: Find out how customers feel about your products
If your company publishes a catalog, let Amazon Comprehend tell you what customers think of your products. Send each customer comment to the `DetectSentiment` operation and it will tell you whether customers feel positive, negative, neutral, or mixed about a product.

Example 3: Discover what matters to your customers
Use Amazon Comprehend topic modeling to discover the topics that your customers are talking about on your forums and message boards, then use entity detection to determine the people, places, and things that they associate with the topic. Finally, use sentiment analysis to determine how your customers feel about a topic.

Benefits

Some of the benefits of using Amazon Comprehend include:

- **Integrate powerful natural language processing into your apps**—Amazon Comprehend removes the complexity of building text analysis capabilities into your applications by making powerful and accurate natural language processing available with a simple API. You don't need textual analysis expertise to take advantage of the insights that Amazon Comprehend produces.

- **Deep learning based natural language processing**—Amazon Comprehend uses deep learning technology to accurately analyze text. Our models are constantly trained with new data across multiple domains to improve accuracy.

- **Scalable natural language processing**—Amazon Comprehend enables you to analyze millions of documents so that you can discover the insights that they contain.

- **Integrate with other AWS services**—Amazon Comprehend is designed to work seamlessly with other AWS services like Amazon S3 and AWS Lambda. Store your documents in Amazon S3, or analyze real-time data with Kinesis Data Firehose. Support for AWS Identity and Access Management (IAM) makes it easy to securely control access to Amazon Comprehend operations. Using IAM, you can create and manage AWS users and groups to grant the appropriate access to your developers and end users.

- **Low cost**—With Amazon Comprehend, you only pay for the documents that you analyze. There are no minimum fees or upfront commitments.

Are You a First-time User of Amazon Comprehend?

If you are a first-time user of Amazon Comprehend, we recommend that you read the following sections in order:

1. **How It Works** – This section introduces Amazon Comprehend concepts.

2. **Getting Started with Amazon Comprehend** – In this section, you set up your account and test Amazon Comprehend.

3. ** API Reference ** – In this section you'll find reference documentation for Amazon Comprehend operations.

How It Works

Amazon Comprehend uses a pre-trained model to examine a document or set of documents to gather insights about the document set. Amazon Comprehend can examine documents in either English or Spanish. The model is continuously trained on a large body of text so that there is no need for you to provide training data. Amazon Comprehend provides the following operations:

- DetectDominantLanguage – to detect the dominant language in a document. Amazon Comprehend can detect 101 different languages.

- DetectEntities – to detect the entities, such as persons or places, in the document.

- DetectKeyPhrases – to detect key noun phrases that are most indicative of the content.

- DetectSentiment – to detect the emotional sentiment, positive, negative, mixed, or neutral, of a document.

- StartTopicsDetectionJob – to detect topics in a set of documents.

All of the operations work on a single document. You can send up to 25 documents in a single batch using the batch operations. When you send a batch, Amazon Comprehend returns a list of responses, one for each document that you sent.

You can use the following batch operations:

- BatchDetectDominantLanguage

- BatchDetectEntities

- BatchDetectKeyPhrases

- BatchDetectSentiment

Topic Modeling

The `StartTopicsDetectionJob` operation starts an asynchronous operation that processes a set of documents stored in an Amazon S3 bucket to determine the topics in the document set. Amazon Comprehend trains its topic model on the corpus of documents that you supply, and then assigns documents and topics based on the insights that it discovered.

Detecting Entities

Use the DetectEntities and BatchDetectEntities operations to detect entities in a document. A *entity* is a textual reference to the unique name of a real-world object such as people, places, and commercial items, and to precise references to measures such as dates and quantities.

For example, in the text "John moved to 1313 Mockingbird Lane in 2012," "John" might be recognized as a PERSON, "1313 Mockingbird Lane" might be recognized as a LOCATION, and "2012" might be recognized as a DATE.

Each entity also has a score that indicates the level of confidence that Amazon Comprehend has that it correctly detected the entity type. You can filter out the entities with lower scores to reduce the risk of using incorrect detections.

The following table lists the entity types.

Type	Description
COMMERCIAL_ITEM	A branded product
DATE	A full date (for example, 11/25/2017), day (Tuesday), month (May), or time (8:30 a.m.)
EVENT	An event, such as a festival, concert, election, etc.
LOCATION	A specific location, such as a country, city, lake, building, etc.
ORGANIZATION	Large organizations, such as a government, company, religion, sports team, etc.
OTHER	Entities that don't fit into any of the other entity categories
PERSON	Individuals, groups of people, nicknames, fictional characters
QUANTITY	A quantified amount, such as currency, percentages, numbers, bytes, etc.
TITLE	An official name given to any creation or creative work, such as movies, books, songs, etc.

Detecting Key Phrases

To determine the key noun phrases used in text, use the Amazon Comprehend DetectKeyPhrases operation. To detect the key noun phrases in up to 25 documents in a batch, use the BatchDetectKeyPhrases operation. For more information, see Using the Batch APIs.

- Detecting Key Phrases Using the AWS Command Line Interface
- Detecting Key Phrases Using the AWS SDK for Java
- Detecting Key Phrases Using the AWS SDK for Python (Boto)

Detecting Key Phrases Using the AWS Command Line Interface

The following example demonstrates using the `DetectKeyPhrases` operation with the AWS CLI. You must specify the language of the input text.

The example is formatted for Unix, Linux, and macOS. For Windows, replace the backslash (\) Unix continuation character at the end of each line with a caret (^).

```
1 aws comprehend detect-key-phrases \
2     --region region \
3     --language-code "en" \
4     --text "It is raining today in Seattle."
```

Amazon Comprehend responds with the following:

```
1 {
2     "LanguageCode": "en",
3     "KeyPhrases": [
4         {
5             "Text": "today",
6             "Score": 0.89,
7             "BeginOffset": 14,
8             "EndOffset": 19
9         },
10        {
11            "Text": "Seattle",
12            "Score": 0.91,
13            "BeginOffset": 23,
14            "EndOffset": 30
15        }
16    ]
17 }
```

Detecting Key Phrases Using the AWS SDK for Java

The following example uses the `DetectKeyPhrases` operation with Java. You must specify the language of the input text.

```
1 import com.amazonaws.auth.AWSCredentialsProvider;
2 import com.amazonaws.auth.DefaultAWSCredentialsProviderChain;
3 import com.amazonaws.services.comprehend.AmazonComprehend;
4 import com.amazonaws.services.comprehend.AmazonComprehendClientBuilder;
5 import com.amazonaws.services.comprehend.model.DetectKeyPhrasesRequest;
6 import com.amazonaws.services.comprehend.model.DetectKeyPhrasesResult;
```

```java
7
8  public class App
9  {
10     public static void main( String[] args )
11     {
12
13         String text = "It is raining today in Seattle";
14
15         // Create credentials using a provider chain. For more information, see
16         // https://docs.aws.amazon.com/sdk-for-java/v1/developer-guide/credentials.html
17         AWSCredentialsProvider awsCreds = DefaultAWSCredentialsProviderChain.getInstance();
18
19         AmazonComprehend comprehendClient =
20             AmazonComprehendClientBuilder.standard()
21                                         .withCredentials(awsCreds)
22                                         .withRegion("region")
23                                         .build();
24
25         // Call detectKeyPhrases API
26         System.out.println("Calling DetectKeyPhrases");
27         DetectKeyPhrasesRequest detectKeyPhrasesRequest = new DetectKeyPhrasesRequest().withText
             (text)
28
                                                                                              .withLangua
                                                                                              ("en
                                                                                              ");
29         DetectKeyPhrasesResult detectKeyPhrasesResult = comprehendClient.detectKeyPhrases(
             detectKeyPhrasesRequest);
30         detectKeyPhrasesResult.getKeyPhrases().forEach(System.out::println);
31         System.out.println("End of DetectKeyPhrases\n");
32     }
33 }
```

Detecting Key Phrases Using the AWS SDK for Python (Boto)

The following example uses the DetectKeyPhrases operation with Python. You must specify the language of the input text.

```python
1  import boto3
2  import json
3
4  comprehend = boto3.client(service_name='comprehend', region_name='region')
5
6  text = "It is raining today in Seattle"
7
8  print('Calling DetectKeyPhrases')
9  print(json.dumps(comprehend.detect_key_phrases(Text=text, LanguageCode='en'), sort_keys=True,
       indent=4))
10 print('End of DetectKeyPhrases\n')
```

Detecting the Primary Language

You can use the DetectDominantLanguage and BatchDetectDominantLanguage operations to examine text to determine the primary language. It identifies the language using identifiers from RFC 5646 — if there is a 2-letter ISO 639-1 identifier, with a regional subtag if necessary, it uses that. Otherwise, it uses the ISO 639-2 3-letter code. For more information about RFC 5646, see Tags for Identifying Languages on the *IETF Tools* web site.

The response includes a score that indicates the confidence level that Amazon Comprehend has that a particular language is the dominant language in the document. Each score is independent of the other scores — it does not indicate that a language makes up a particular percentage of a document.

If a long document, like a book, is written in multiple languages, you can break the long document into smaller pieces and run the `DetectDominantLanguage` operation on the individual pieces. You can then aggregate the results to determine the percentage of each language in the longer document.

Amazon Comprehend can detect the following languages.

Code	Language	Code	Language	Code	Language
af	Afrikaans	hy	Armenian	ps	Pushto
am	Amharic	ilo	Iloko	qu	Quechua
ar	Arabic	id	Indonesian	ro	Romanian
as	Assamese	is	Icelandic	ru	Russian
az	Azerbaijani	it	Italian	sa	Sanskrit
ba	Bashkir	jv	Javanese	si	Sinhala
be	Belarusian	ja	Japanese	sk	Slovak
bn	Bengali	kn	Kannada	sl	Slovenian
bs	Bosnian	ka	Georgian	sd	Sindhi
bg	Bulgarian	kk	Kazakh	so	Somali
ca	Catalan	km	Central Khmer	es	Spanish
ceb	Cebuano	ky	Kirghiz	sq	Albanian
cs	Czech	ko	Korean	sr	Serbian
cv	Chuvash	ku	Kurdish	su	Sundanese
cy	Welsh	la	Latin	sw	Swahili
da	Danish	lv	Latvian	sv	Swedish
de	German	lt	Lithuanian	ta	Tamil
el	Greek	lb	Luxembourgish	tt	Tatar
en	English	ml	Malayalam	te	Telugu
eo	Esperanto	mr	Marathi	tg	Tajik
et	Estonian	mk	Macedonian	tl	Tagalog
eu	Basque	mg	Malagasy	th	Thai
fa	Persian	mn	Mongolian	tk	Turkmen
fi	Finnish	ms	Malay	tr	Turkish
fr	French	my	Burmese	ug	Uighur
gd	Scottish Gaelic	ne	Nepali	uk	Ukrainian
ga	Irish	new	Newari	ur	Urdu
gl	Galician	nl	Dutch	uz	Uzbek
gu	Gujarati	no	Norwegian	vi	Vietnamese
ht	Haitian	or	Oriya	yi	Yiddish
he	Hebrew	pa	Punjabi	yo	Yoruba
hi	Hindi	pl	Polish	zh	Chinese (Simplified)
hr	Croatian	pt	Portuguese	zh-TW	Chinese (Traditional)
hu	Hungarian				

Detecting Sentiments

Use Amazon Comprehend to determine the sentiment of a document. You can determine if the sentiment is positive, negative, neutral, or mixed. For example, you can use sentiment analysis to determine the sentiments of comments on a blog posting to determine if your readers liked the post.

The DetectSentiment and BatchDetectSentiment operations return the most likely sentiment for the text as well as the scores for each of the sentiments. The score represents the likelihood that the sentiment was correctly detected. For example, in the first example below it is 95 percent likely that the text has a `Positive` sentiment. There is a less than 1 percent likelihood that the text has a `Negative` sentiment. You can use the `SentimentScore` to determine if the accuracy of the detection meets the needs of your application.

The following examples show the input text and output from the `DetectSentiment` operation. The examples are formatted for Unix, Linux, and macOS. For Windows, replace the backslash (\) Unix continuation character at the end of each line with a caret (^).

Positive sentiment:

```
1 aws comprehend detect-sentiment \
2     --endpoint-url endpoint \
3     --region region \
4     --language-code "en" \
5     --text "I feel great this morning."
6 {
7     "SentimentScore": {
8         "Mixed": 0.008924853056669235,
9         "Positive": 0.9584325551986694,
10        "Neutral": 0.026196759194135666,
11        "Negative": 0.006445900071412325
12    },
13    "Sentiment": "POSITIVE",
14 }
```

Negative sentiment:

```
1 aws comprehend detect-sentiment \
2     --endpoint-url endpoint \
3     --region region \
4     --language-code "en" \
5     --text "This view is horrible."
6 {
7     "SentimentScore": {
8         "Mixed": 0.024891886860132217,
9         "Positive": 0.050186172127723694,
10        "Neutral": 0.1579618602991104,
11        "Negative": 0.7669601440429688
12    },
13    "Sentiment": "NEGATIVE",
14 }
```

Neutral sentiment:

```
1 aws comprehend detect-sentiment \
2     --endpoint-url endpoint \
3     --region region \
4     --language-code "en" \
5     --text "Childhood is the time to play"
```

```
 6 {
 7     "SentimentScore": {
 8         "Mixed": 0.020051531493663788,
 9         "Positive": 0.35540205240249634,
10         "Neutral": 0.4203023612499237,
11         "Negative": 0.20424406230449677
12     },
13     "Sentiment": "NEUTRAL",
14 }
```

Mixed sentiment:

```
 1 aws comprehend detect-sentiment \
 2     --endpoint-url endpoint \
 3     --region region \
 4     --language-code "en" \
 5     --text "I love Seattle but the winter is too cold for me."
 6 {
 7     "SentimentScore": {
 8         "Mixed": 0.5408428907394409,
 9         "Positive": 0.25948983430862427,
10         "Neutral": 0.06789177656173706,
11         "Negative": 0.13177546858787537
12     },
13     "Sentiment": "MIXED",
14 }
```

Batch Processing Documents

When you have multiple documents that you want to process, you can use batch operations to send more than one document to Amazon Comprehend at a time. You can send up to 25 documents in each batch. Amazon Comprehend sends back a list of responses, one for each document in the batch.

Using the batch operations is identical to calling the single document APIs for each of the documents in the request. Calling the batch APIs can result in better performance for your applications.

The input to the batch APIs is a JSON structure containing the documents to process. For all operations except BatchDetectDominantLanguage, you must set the input language. You can set only one input language for each batch. For example, the following is the input to the BatchDetectEntities operation. It contains two documents and is in English.

```
1  {
2    "LanguageCode": "en",
3    "TextList": [
4       "I have been living in Seattle for almost 4 years",
5       "It is raining today in Seattle"
6    ]
7  }
```

The response from a batch operation contains two lists, the ResultList and the ErrorList. The ResultList contains one record for each document that was successfully processed. The result for each document in the batch is identical to the result you would get if you ran a single document operation on the document. The results for each document are assigned an index based on the order of the documents in the input file. The response from the BatchDetectEntities operation is:

```
1  {
2    "ResultList" : [
3       {
4          "Index": 0,
5          "Entities": [
6             {
7                "Text": "Seattle",
8                "Score": 0.95,
9                "Type": "LOCATION",
10               "BeginOffset": 22,
11               "EndOffset": 29
12            },
13            {
14               "Text": "almost 4 years",
15               "Score": 0.89,
16               "Type": "QUANTITY",
17               "BeginOffset": 34,
18               "EndOffset": 48
19            }
20         ]
21      },
22      {
23         "Index": 1,
24         "Entities": [
25            {
26               "Text": "today",
27               "Score": 0.87,
28               "Type": "DATE",
```

```
29            "BeginOffset": 14,
30            "EndOffset": 19
31          },
32          {
33            "Text": "Seattle",
34            "Score": 0.96,
35            "Type": "LOCATION",
36            "BeginOffset": 23,
37            "EndOffset": 30
38          }
39        ]
40      }
41    ],
42    "ErrorList": []
43 }
```

When an error occurs in the batch request the response contains an `ErrorList` that identifies the documents that contained an error. The document is identified by its index in the input list. For example, the following input to the `BatchDetectLanguage` operation contains a document that cannot be processed:

```
1 {
2    "TextList": [
3      "hello friend",
4      "$$$$$$",
5      "hola amigo"
6    ]
7 }
```

The response from Amazon Comprehend includes an error list that identifies the document that contained an error:

```
1 {
2    "ResultList": [
3      {
4        "Index": 0,
5        "Languages":[
6          {
7            "LanguageCode":"en",
8            "Score": 0.99
9          }
10       ]
11     },
12     {
13       "Index": 2
14       "Languages":[
15         {
16           "LanguageCode":"es",
17           "Score": 0.82
18         }
19       ]
20     }
21   ],
22   "ErrorList": [
23     {
24       "Index": 1,
25       "ErrorCode": "InternalServerException",
```

```
26        "ErrorMessage": "Unexpected Server Error. Please try again."
27      }
28    ]
29 }
```

Topic Modeling

To determine the topics in a document set, use the StartTopicsDetectionJob to start an asynchronous job.

- Before You Start
- Topic Modeling Using the AWS Command Line Interface
- Topic Modeling Using the AWS SDK for Java
- Topic Modeling Using the AWS SDK for Python (Boto)

Before You Start

Before you start, make sure that you have:

- **Input and output buckets**—Identify the Amazon S3 buckets that you want to use for input and output. The buckets must be in the same region as the API that you are calling.

- **IAM service role**—You must have an IAM service role with permission to access your input and output buckets. For more information, see Role-Based Permissions Required for Topic Detection.

Topic Modeling Using the AWS Command Line Interface

The following example demonstrates using the `StartTopicsDetectionJob` operation with the AWS CLI

The example is formatted for Unix, Linux, and macOS. For Windows, replace the backslash (\\) Unix continuation character at the end of each line with a caret (^).

```
1 aws comprehend start-topics-detection-job \
2                  --number-of-topics topics to return \
3                  --job-name "job name" \
4                  --region region \
5                  --cli-input-json file://path to JSON input file
```

For the `cli-input-json` parameter you supply the path to a JSON file that contains the request data, as shown in the following example.

```
1 {
2     "InputDataConfig": {
3         "S3Uri": "s3://input bucket/input path",
4         "InputFormat": "ONE_DOC_PER_FILE"
5     },
6     "OutputDataConfig": {
7         "S3Uri": "s3://output bucket/output path"
8     },
9     "DataAccessRoleArn": "arn:aws:iam::account ID:role/data access role"
10 }
```

If the request to start the topic detection job was successful, you will receive the following response:

```
1 {
2     "JobStatus": "SUBMITTED",
3     "JobId": "job ID"
4 }
```

Use the ListTopicsDetectionJobs operation to see a list of the topic detection jobs that you have submitted. The list includes information about the input and output locations that you used as well as the status of each of the detection jobs. The example is formatted for Unix, Linux, and macOS. For Windows, replace the backslash (\) Unix continuation character at the end of each line with a caret (^).

```
1 aws comprehend list-topics-detection-jobs \
2     -- region
```

You will get JSON similar to the following in response:

```
1  {
2      "TopicsDetectionJobPropertiesList": [
3          {
4              "InputDataConfig": {
5                  "S3Uri": "s3://input bucket/input path",
6                  "InputFormat": "ONE_DOC_PER_LINE"
7              },
8              "NumberOfTopics": topics to return,
9              "JobId": "job ID",
10             "JobStatus": "COMPLETED",
11             "JobName": "job name",
12             "SubmitTime": timestamp,
13             "OutputDataConfig": {
14                 "S3Uri": "s3://output bucket/output path"
15             },
16             "EndTime": timestamp
17         },
18         {
19             "InputDataConfig": {
20                 "S3Uri": "s3://input bucket/input path",
21                 "InputFormat": "ONE_DOC_PER_LINE"
22             },
23             "NumberOfTopics": topics to return,
24             "JobId": "job ID",
25             "JobStatus": "RUNNING",
26             "JobName": "job name",
27             "SubmitTime": timestamp,
28             "OutputDataConfig": {
29                 "S3Uri": "s3://output bucket/output path"
30             }
31         }
32     ]
33 }
```

You can use the DescribeTopicsDetectionJob operation to get the status of an existing job. The example is formatted for Unix, Linux, and macOS. For Windows, replace the backslash (\) Unix continuation character at the end of each line with a caret (^).

```
1 aws comprehend describe-topics-detection-job
2                --region region \
3                --job-id job ID
4 I
```

You will get the following JSON in response:

```
1 {
2     "TopicsDetectionJobProperties": {
3         "InputDataConfig": {
4             "S3Uri": "s3://input bucket/input path",
```

```
 5          "InputFormat": "ONE_DOC_PER_LINE"
 6       },
 7       "NumberOfTopics": topics to return,
 8       "JobId": "job ID",
 9       "JobStatus": "COMPLETED",
10       "JobName": "job name",
11       "SubmitTime": timestamp,
12       "OutputDataConfig": {
13           "S3Uri": "s3://output bucket/ouput path"
14       },
15       "EndTime": timestamp
16    }
17 }
```

Topic Modeling Using the AWS SDK for Java

The following Java program detects the topics in a document collection. It uses the StartTopicsDetectionJob operation to start detecting topics. Next, it uses the DescribeTopicsDetectionJob operation to check the status of the topic detection. Finally, it calls ListTopicsDetectionJobs to show a list of all jobs submitted for the account.

```java
 1 import com.amazonaws.auth.AWSCredentialsProvider;
 2 import com.amazonaws.auth.DefaultAWSCredentialsProviderChain;
 3 import com.amazonaws.client.builder.AwsClientBuilder;
 4 import com.amazonaws.services.comprehend.AmazonComprehend;
 5 import com.amazonaws.services.comprehend.AmazonComprehendClientBuilder;
 6 import com.amazonaws.services.comprehend.model.DescribeTopicsDetectionJobRequest;
 7 import com.amazonaws.services.comprehend.model.DescribeTopicsDetectionJobResult;
 8 import com.amazonaws.services.comprehend.model.InputDataConfig;
 9 import com.amazonaws.services.comprehend.model.InputFormat;
10 import com.amazonaws.services.comprehend.model.ListTopicsDetectionJobsRequest;
11 import com.amazonaws.services.comprehend.model.ListTopicsDetectionJobsResult;
12 import com.amazonaws.services.comprehend.model.StartTopicsDetectionJobRequest;
13 import com.amazonaws.services.comprehend.model.StartTopicsDetectionJobResult;
14
15 public class App
16 {
17     public static void main( String[] args )
18     {
19         // Create credentials using a provider chain. For more information, see
20         // https://docs.aws.amazon.com/sdk-for-java/v1/developer-guide/credentials.html
21         AWSCredentialsProvider awsCreds = DefaultAWSCredentialsProviderChain.getInstance();
22
23         AmazonComprehend comprehendClient =
24             AmazonComprehendClientBuilder.standard()
25                                          .withCredentials(awsCreds)
26                                          .withRegion("region")
27                                          .build();
28
29         final String inputS3Uri = "s3://input bucket/input path";
30         final InputFormat inputDocFormat = InputFormat.ONE_DOC_PER_FILE;
31         final String outputS3Uri = "s3://output bucket/output path";
32         final String dataAccessRoleArn = "arn:aws:iam::account ID:role/data access role";
33         final int numberOfTopics = 10;
34
```

```
35    final StartTopicsDetectionJobRequest startTopicsDetectionJobRequest = new
          StartTopicsDetectionJobRequest()
36            .withInputDataConfig(new InputDataConfig()
37                    .withS3Uri(inputS3Uri)
38                    .withInputFormat(inputDocFormat))
39            .withOutputDataConfig(new OutputDataConfig()
40                    .withS3Uri(outputS3Uri))
41            .withDataAccessRoleArn(dataAccessRoleArn)
42            .withNumberOfTopics(numberOfTopics);
43
44    final StartTopicsDetectionJobResult startTopicsDetectionJobResult = comprehendClient.
          startTopicsDetectionJob(startTopicsDetectionJobRequest);
45
46    final String jobId = startTopicsDetectionJobResult.getJobId();
47    System.out.println("JobId: " + jobId);
48
49    final DescribeTopicsDetectionJobRequest describeTopicsDetectionJobRequest = new
          DescribeTopicsDetectionJobRequest()
50            .withJobId(jobId);
51
52    final DescribeTopicsDetectionJobResult describeTopicsDetectionJobResult =
          comprehendClient.describeTopicsDetectionJob(describeTopicsDetectionJobRequest);
53    System.out.println("describeTopicsDetectionJobResult: " +
          describeTopicsDetectionJobResult);
54
55    ListTopicsDetectionJobsResult listTopicsDetectionJobsResult = comprehendClient.
          listTopicsDetectionJobs(new ListTopicsDetectionJobsRequest());
56    System.out.println("listTopicsDetectionJobsResult: " + listTopicsDetectionJobsResult);
57
58    }
59 }
```

Topic Modeling Using the AWS SDK for Python (Boto)

The following Python program detects the topics in a document collection. It uses the StartTopicsDetectionJob operation to start detecting topics. Next, it uses the DescribeTopicsDetectionJob operation to check the status of the topic detection. Finally, it calls ListTopicsDetectionJobs to show a list of all jobs submitted for the account.

```
1 import boto3
2 import json
3 from bson import json_util
4
5 comprehend = boto3.client(service_name='comprehend', region_name='region')
6
7 input_s3_url = "s3://input bucket/input path"
8 input_doc_format = "ONE_DOC_PER_FILE"
9 output_s3_url = "s3://output bucket/output path"
10 data_access_role_arn = "arn:aws:iam::account ID:role/data access role"
11 number_of_topics = 10
12
13 input_data_config = {"S3Uri": input_s3_url, "InputFormat": input_doc_format}
14 output_data_config = {"S3Uri": output_s3_url}
15
```

```
16  start_topics_detection_job_result = comprehend.start_topics_detection_job(NumberOfTopics=
        number_of_topics,
17                                                              InputDataConfig=
                                                                  input_data_config
                                                                  ,
18                                                              OutputDataConfig=
                                                                  output_data_config
                                                                  ,
19                                                              DataAccessRoleArn=
                                                                  data_access_role_ar
                                                                  )
20
21  print('start_topics_detection_job_result: ' + json.dumps(start_topics_detection_job_result))
22
23  job_id = start_topics_detection_job_result["JobId"]
24
25  print('job_id: ' + job_id)
26
27  describe_topics_detection_job_result = comprehend.describe_topics_detection_job(JobId=job_id)
28
29  print('describe_topics_detection_job_result: ' + json.dumps(describe_topics_detection_job_result
        , default=json_util.default))
30
31  list_topics_detection_jobs_result = comprehend.list_topics_detection_jobs()
32
33  print('list_topics_detection_jobs_result: ' + json.dumps(list_topics_detection_jobs_result,
        default=json_util.default))
```

Getting Started with Amazon Comprehend

To get started using Amazon Comprehend, set up an AWS account and create an AWS Identity and Access Management (IAM) user. To use the AWS Command Line Interface (AWS CLI), download and configure it.

- Step 1: Set Up an AWS Account and Create an Administrator User
- Step 2: Set Up the AWS Command Line Interface (AWS CLI)
- Step 3: Getting Started Using the Amazon Comprehend Console
- Step 4: Getting Started Using the Amazon Comprehend API

Step 1: Set Up an AWS Account and Create an Administrator User

Before you use Amazon Comprehend for the first time, complete the following tasks:

1. Sign Up for AWS

2. Create an IAM User

Sign Up for AWS

When you sign up for Amazon Web Services (AWS), your AWS account is automatically signed up for all AWS services, including Amazon Comprehend. You are charged only for the services that you use.

With Amazon Comprehend, you pay only for the resources that you use. If you are a new AWS customer, you can get started with Amazon Comprehend for free. For more information, see AWS Free Usage Tier.

If you already have an AWS account, skip to the next section.

To create an AWS account

1. Open https://aws.amazon.com/, and then choose **Create an AWS Account**. **Note**
   This might be unavailable in your browser if you previously signed into the AWS Management Console. In that case, choose **Sign in to a different account**, and then choose **Create a new AWS account**.

2. Follow the online instructions.

   Part of the sign-up procedure involves receiving a phone call and entering a PIN using the phone keypad.

Record your AWS account ID because you'll need it for the next task.

Create an IAM User

Services in AWS, such as Amazon Comprehend, require that you provide credentials when you access them. This allows the service to determine whether you have permissions to access the service's resources.

We strongly recommend that you access AWS using AWS Identity and Access Management (IAM), not the credentials for your AWS account. To use IAM to access AWS, create an IAM user, add the user to an IAM group with administrative permissions, and then grant administrative permissions to the IAM user. You can then access AWS using a special URL and the IAM user's credentials.

The Getting Started exercises in this guide assume that you have a user with administrator privileges, `adminuser`.

To create an administrator user and sign in to the console

1. Create an administrator user called `adminuser` in your AWS account. For instructions, see Creating Your First IAM User and Administrators Group in the *IAM User Guide*.

2. Sign in to the AWS Management Console using a special URL. For more information, see How Users Sign In to Your Account in the *IAM User Guide*.

For more information about IAM, see the following:

- AWS Identity and Access Management (IAM)

- Getting Started

- IAM User Guide

Next Step

Step 2: Set Up the AWS Command Line Interface (AWS CLI)

Step 2: Set Up the AWS Command Line Interface (AWS CLI)

You don't need the AWS CLI to perform the steps in the Getting Started exercises. However, some of the other exercises in this guide do require it. If you prefer, you can skip this step and go to Step 3: Getting Started Using the Amazon Comprehend Console, and set up the AWS CLI later.

To set up the AWS CLI

1. Download and configure the AWS CLI. For instructions, see the following topics in the *AWS Command Line Interface User Guide*:

   - Getting Set Up with the AWS Command Line Interface

   - Configuring the AWS Command Line Interface

2. In the AWS CLI config file, add a named profile for the administrator user:.

```
1 [profile adminuser]
2 aws_access_key_id = adminuser access key ID
3 aws_secret_access_key = adminuser secret access key
4 region = aws-region
```

   You use this profile when executing the AWS CLI commands. For more information about named profiles, see Named Profiles in the *AWS Command Line Interface User Guide*. For a list of AWS Regions, see Regions and Endpoints in the *Amazon Web Services General Reference*.

3. Verify the setup by typing the following help command at the command prompt:

```
1 aws help
```

Next Step

Step 3: Getting Started Using the Amazon Comprehend Console

Step 3: Getting Started Using the Amazon Comprehend Console

The easiest way to get started using Amazon Comprehend is to use the console to analyze a short text file. If you haven't reviewed the concepts and terminology in How It Works, we recommend that you do that before proceeding.

- Analyzing Documents Using the Console
- Creating a Topic Modeling Job Using the Console

Next Step
Step 4: Getting Started Using the Amazon Comprehend API

Analyzing Documents Using the Console

The Amazon Comprehend console enables you to analyze the contents of documents up to 1,000 characters long. The results are shown in the console so that you can review the analysis.

To start analyzing documents, sign in to the AWS Management Console and open the Amazon Comprehend console.

The console displays sample text and the analysis of that text:

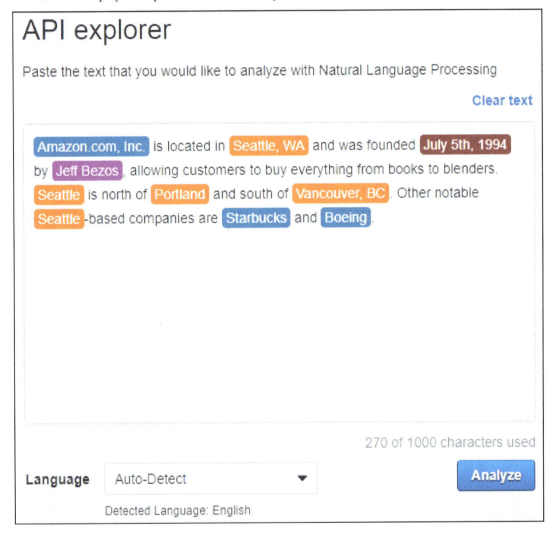

You can replace the sample text with your own text and then choose **Analyze** to get an analysis of your text.

The text is color-coded to indicate the entity type of significant words:

- Orange tags identify locations.
- Brown tags identify dates.
- Magenta tags identify persons.
- Blue tags identify organizations.
- Black tags identify other entities that don't fit into any of the other entity categories.

For more information, see Detecting Entities

On the right side of the console, the **Analysis** pane shows more information about the text.

The **Entity** section displays cards for the entities found in the text:

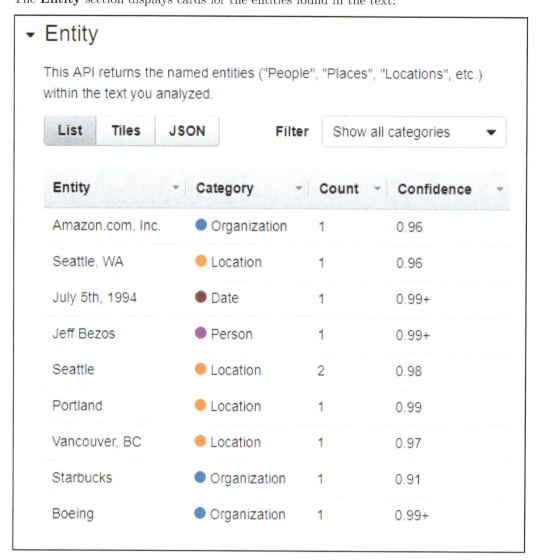

Each card shows the text and its entity type. To see a list of all of the entities in the text, choose **List**. For a JSON structure of the results, choose **JSON**. The JSON structure is the same as the structure returned by the DetectEntities operation.

The **Key phrases** section of the **Analysis** pane lists key noun phrases that Amazon Comprehend detected in the input text. For the sample input text, the **Key phrases** section looks like this:

▾ Key phrases

This API returns the key phrases and a confidence score to support that this is a key phrase.

Key phrase ▾	Count ▾	Confidence ▾
Amazon.com	1	0.88
Seattle, WA	1	0.98
July 5th	1	0.94
1994	1	0.99
Jeff Bezos	1	0.99+
customers	1	0.99
books	1	0.99+
blenders	1	0.99
Seattle	1	0.99+
Portland	1	0.72
Vancouver, BC	1	0.88

Show all

For an alternative view of the results, choose **List** or **JSON** . The JSON structure is the same as the one returned by the DetectKeyPhrases operation.

The **Language** section shows the dominant language for the sample text and the Confidence score. The Confidence score represents the level of confidence that Amazon Comprehend has that it's detected the dominant language correctly. Amazon Comprehend can recognize 100 languages. For more information, see Detecting the Primary Language .

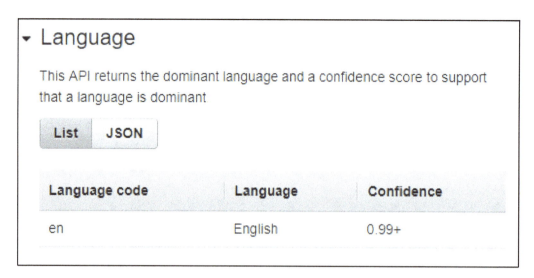

As with the other sections, you can choose **List** or **JSON** to get another view of the results. The JSON structure is the same as the one returned by the DetectDominantLanguage operation.

The **Sentiment** section of the **Analysis** pane shows the overall emotional sentiment of the text.

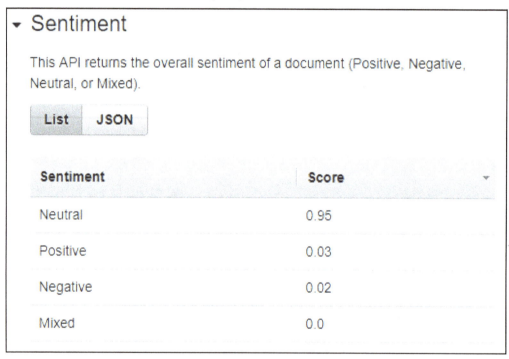

The score represents the confidence that Amazon Comprehend has that it has correctly detected the emotional sentiment expressed in the text. Sentiment can be rated positive, neutral, mixed, or negative.

Creating a Topic Modeling Job Using the Console

You can use the Amazon Comprehend console to create and manage asynchronous topic detection jobs.

To create a topic detection job

1. Sign in to the AWS Management Console and open the Amazon Comprehend console.

2. From the left menu, choose **Topic Modeling** and then choose **Create**.

3. Choose the data source to use. You can use either sample data or you can analyze your own data stored in an Amazon S3 bucket. If you use the sample dataset, the topic modeling job analyzes text from this collection of articles: https://s3.amazonaws.com/public-sample-attributions/Attributions.txt

4. If you chose to use your own data, provide the following information in the **Choose input data** section:

   - **S3 data location** – An Amazon S3 data bucket that contains the documents to analyze. You can choose the folder icon to browse to the location of your data. The bucket must be in the same region as the API that you are calling.

   - **Input format** – Choose whether in input data is contained in one document per file, or if there is one document per line in a file.

   - **Number of topics** – The number of topics to return.

   - **Job name** – A name that identifies the particular job.

5. In the **Choose output location** section, provide the following:

   - **S3 data location** – an Amazon S3 data bucket where the results of the analysis will be written. The bucket must be in the same region as the API that your are calling.

6. In the **Choose an IAM role** section, either select an existing IAM role or create a new one.

   - **Choose an existing IAM role** – Choose this option if you already have an IAM role with permissions to access the input and output Amazon S3 buckets.

   - **Create a new IAM role** – Choose this option when you want to create a new IAM role with the proper permissions for Amazon Comprehend to access the input and output buckets. For more information about the permissions given to the IAM role, see Role-Based Permissions Required for Topic Detection.

7. When you have finished filling out the form, choose **Create job** to create and start the topic detection job.

Select input data

Please select the topic modeling data you would like to analyze. Our text analytics services work best when there are at least 1,000 documents of at least 100 words each, but can be applied to documents of any size up to 1MB, and from 10's to millions of documents.

- ● Topic modeling sample data
- ○ My data (S3)

S3 data location   s3://public-sample-us-west-2   📂 ❶

Input format   One document per line   ▼ ❶

Number of topics   10   ❶

Job Name   <job name>   ❶

Any characters; length between 1-256

Select output location

Select the preferred output format for your analysis. S3 data output location, and the format of data as CSV.

S3 data location   s3://<output bucket>   📂 ❶

Select an IAM role

The topic modeling job will use the IAM role to access your Amazon S3 input and output buckets.

- ○ Select an existing IAM role
- ● Create a new IAM role

Name suffix   <IAM role name>   ❶

Your roles will be prefixed with "AmazonComprehendServiceRole-". By clicking "Create job" you are authorizing creation of this role.

Cancel   **Create job**

The new job appears in the job list with the status field showing the status of the job. The field can be IN_PROGRESS for a job that is processing, COMPLETED for a job that has finished successfully, and FAILED for a job that has an error. You can click on a job to get more information about the job, including any error messages.

Job info

Job name	TestModelingData
Job ID	e2e6b85584b3c5a48634ce2e8497c864
Analysis type	Topic modeling
Number of topics	10
Start time	28 Nov 2017 03:21:09 GMT
End time	--
Status	IN_PROGRESS
Job information	--

Actions

Input data location	s3://public-sample-us-west-2
Output data location	s3://test-comprehend/e2e6b85584b3c5a48634ce2e8497c864-1511839269301/output/output.tar.gz

Step 4: Getting Started Using the Amazon Comprehend API

The following examples demonstrate how to use Amazon Comprehend operations using the AWS CLI, Java, and Python. Use them to learn about Amazon Comprehend operations and as building blocks for your own applications.

To run the AWS CLI and Python examples, you need to install the AWS CLI. For more information, see Step 2: Set Up the AWS Command Line Interface (AWS CLI).

To run the Java examples, you need to install the AWS SDK for Java. For instructions for installing the SDK for Java, see Set up the AWS SDK for Java.

- Detecting the Dominant Language
- Detecting Named Entities
- Detecting Key Phrases
- Detecting Sentiment
- Topic Modeling
- Using the Batch APIs

Detecting the Dominant Language

To determine the dominant language used in text, use the Amazon Comprehend DetectDominantLanguage operation. To detect the dominant language in up to 25 documents in a batch, use the BatchDetectDominantLanguage operation. For more information, see Using the Batch APIs.

- Detecting the Dominant Language Using the AWS Command Line Interface
- Detecting the Dominant Language Using the AWS SDK for Java
- Detecting the Dominant Language Using the AWS SDK for Python (Boto)

Detecting the Dominant Language Using the AWS Command Line Interface

The following example demonstrates using the `DetectDominantLanguage` operation with the AWS CLI.

The example is formatted for Unix, Linux, and macOS. For Windows, replace the backslash (\) Unix continuation character at the end of each line with a caret (^).

```
1  aws comprehend detect-dominant-language \
2      --region region \
3      --text "It is raining today in Seattle."
```

Amazon Comprehend responds with the following:

```
1  {
2      "Languages": [
3          {
4              "LanguageCode": "en",
5              "Score": 0.9793661236763
6          }
7      ]
8  }
```

Detecting the Dominant Language Using the AWS SDK for Java

The following example uses the `DetectDominantLanguage` operation with Java.

```
1  import com.amazonaws.auth.AWSCredentialsProvider;
2  import com.amazonaws.auth.DefaultAWSCredentialsProviderChain;
3  import com.amazonaws.services.comprehend.AmazonComprehend;
4  import com.amazonaws.services.comprehend.AmazonComprehendClientBuilder;
5  import com.amazonaws.services.comprehend.model.DetectDominantLanguageRequest;
6  import com.amazonaws.services.comprehend.model.DetectDominantLanguageResult;
7
8  public class App
9  {
10     public static void main( String[] args )
11     {
12
13         String text = "It is raining today in Seattle";
14
15         // Create credentials using a provider chain. For more information, see
16         // https://docs.aws.amazon.com/sdk-for-java/v1/developer-guide/credentials.html
17         AWSCredentialsProvider awsCreds = DefaultAWSCredentialsProviderChain.getInstance();
18
```

```
19    AmazonComprehend comprehendClient =
20        AmazonComprehendClientBuilder.standard()
21                            .withCredentials(awsCreds)
22                            .withRegion("region")
23                            .build();
24
25    // Call detectDominantLanguage API
26    System.out.println("Calling DetectDominantLanguage");
27    DetectDominantLanguageRequest detectDominantLanguageRequest = new
           DetectDominantLanguageRequest().withText(text);
28    DetectDominantLanguageResult detectDominantLanguageResult = comprehendClient.
           detectDominantLanguage(detectDominantLanguageRequest);
29    detectDominantLanguageResult.getLanguages().forEach(System.out::println);
30    System.out.println("Calling DetectDominantLanguage\n");
31    System.out.println("Done");
32  }
33 }
```

Detecting the Dominant Language Using the AWS SDK for Python (Boto)

The following example demonstrates using the DetectDominantLanguage operation with Python.

```
1 import boto3
2 import json
3
4 comprehend = boto3.client(service_name='comprehend', region_name='region')
5 text = "It is raining today in Seattle"
6
7 print('Calling DetectDominantLanguage')
8 print(json.dumps(comprehend.detect_dominant_language(Text = text), sort_keys=True, indent=4))
9 print("End of DetectDominantLanguage\n")
```

Detecting Named Entities

To determine the named entities in a document, use the Amazon Comprehend DetectEntities operation. To detect entities in up to 25 documents in a batch, use the BatchDetectEntities operation. For more information, see Using the Batch APIs.

- Detecting Named Entities Using the AWS Command Line Interface
- Detecting Named Entities Using the AWS SDK for Java
- Detecting Named Entities Using the AWS SDK for Python (Boto)

Detecting Named Entities Using the AWS Command Line Interface

The following example demonstrates using the `DetectEntities` operation using the AWS CLI. You must specify the language of the input text.

The example is formatted for Unix, Linux, and macOS. For Windows, replace the backslash (\) Unix continuation character at the end of each line with a caret (^).

```
aws comprehend detect-entities \
    --region region \
    --language-code "en" \
    --text "It is raining today in Seattle."
```

Amazon Comprehend responds with the following:

```
{
    "Entities": [
        {
            "Text": "today",
            "Score": 0.97,
            "Type": "DATE",
            "BeginOffset": 14,
            "EndOffset": 19
        },
        {
            "Text": "Seattle",
            "Score": 0.95,
            "Type": "LOCATION",
            "BeginOffset": 23,
            "EndOffset": 30
        }
    ],
    "LanguageCode": "en"
}
```

Detecting Named Entities Using the AWS SDK for Java

The following example uses the `DetectEntities` operation with Java. You must specify the language of the input text.

```
import com.amazonaws.auth.AWSCredentialsProvider;
import com.amazonaws.auth.DefaultAWSCredentialsProviderChain;
import com.amazonaws.services.comprehend.AmazonComprehend;
import com.amazonaws.services.comprehend.AmazonComprehendClientBuilder;
```

```
 5  import com.amazonaws.services.comprehend.model.DetectEntitiesRequest;
 6  import com.amazonaws.services.comprehend.model.DetectEntitiesResult;
 7
 8  public class App
 9  {
10      public static void main( String[] args )
11      {
12
13          String text = "It is raining today in Seattle";
14
15          // Create credentials using a provider chain. For more information, see
16          // https://docs.aws.amazon.com/sdk-for-java/v1/developer-guide/credentials.html
17          AWSCredentialsProvider awsCreds = DefaultAWSCredentialsProviderChain.getInstance();
18
19          AmazonComprehend comprehendClient =
20              AmazonComprehendClientBuilder.standard()
21                                          .withCredentials(awsCreds)
22                                          .withRegion("region")
23                                          .build();
24
25          // Call detectEntities API
26          System.out.println("Calling DetectEntities");
27          DetectEntitiesRequest detectEntitiesRequest = new DetectEntitiesRequest().withText(text)
28                                                                                   .
                                                                        withLanguageCode
                                                                        ("en");
29          DetectEntitiesResult detectEntitiesResult  = comprehendClient.detectEntities(
                  detectEntitiesRequest);
30          detectEntitiesResult.getEntities().forEach(System.out::println);
31          System.out.println("End of DetectEntities\n");
32      }
33  }
```

Detecting Named Entities Using the AWS SDK for Python (Boto)

The following example uses the DetectEntities operation with Python. You must specify the language of the input text.

```
1  import boto3
2  import json
3
4  comprehend = boto3.client(service_name='comprehend', region_name='region')
5  text = "It is raining today in Seattle"
6
7  print('Calling DetectEntities')
8  print(json.dumps(comprehend.detect_entities(Text=text, LanguageCode='en'), sort_keys=True,
       indent=4))
9  print('End of DetectEntities\n')
```

Detecting Sentiment

To determine the overall emotional tone of text, use the DetectSentiment operation. To detect the sentiment in up to 25 documents in a batch, use the BatchDetectSentiment operation. For more information, see Using the Batch APIs.

- Detecting Sentiment Using the AWS Command Line Interface
- Detecting Sentiment Using the AWS SDK for Java
- Detecting Sentiment Using the AWS SDK for Python (Boto)

Detecting Sentiment Using the AWS Command Line Interface

The following example demonstrates using the `DetectSentiment` operation with the AWS CLI. This example specifies the language of the input text.

The example is formatted for Unix, Linux, and macOS. For Windows, replace the backslash (\) Unix continuation character at the end of each line with a caret (^).

```
1 aws comprehend detect-sentiment \
2     --region region \
3     --language-code "en" \
4     --text "It is raining today in Seattle."
```

Amazon Comprehend responds with the following:

```
1  {
2      "SentimentScore": {
3          "Mixed": 0.014585512690246105,
4          "Positive": 0.31592071056365967,
5          "Neutral": 0.5985543131828308,
6          "Negative": 0.07093945890665054
7      },
8      "Sentiment": "NEUTRAL",
9      "LanguageCode": "en"
10 }
```

Detecting Sentiment Using the AWS SDK for Java

The following example Java program detects the sentiment of input text. You must specify the language of the input text.

```
1  import com.amazonaws.auth.AWSCredentialsProvider;
2  import com.amazonaws.auth.DefaultAWSCredentialsProviderChain;
3  import com.amazonaws.services.comprehend.AmazonComprehend;
4  import com.amazonaws.services.comprehend.AmazonComprehendClientBuilder;
5  import com.amazonaws.services.comprehend.model.DetectSentimentRequest;
6  import com.amazonaws.services.comprehend.model.DetectSentimentResult;
7
8  public class App
9  {
10     public static void main( String[] args )
11     {
12
13         String text = "It is raining today in Seattle";
```

39

```
14
15        // Create credentials using a provider chain. For more information, see
16        // https://docs.aws.amazon.com/sdk-for-java/v1/developer-guide/credentials.html
17        AWSCredentialsProvider awsCreds = DefaultAWSCredentialsProviderChain.getInstance();
18
19        AmazonComprehend comprehendClient =
20            AmazonComprehendClientBuilder.standard()
21                                    .withCredentials(awsCreds)
22                                    .withRegion("region")
23                                    .build();
24
25        // Call detectSentiment API
26        System.out.println("Calling DetectSentiment");
27        DetectSentimentRequest detectSentimentRequest = new DetectSentimentRequest().withText(
            text)
28
                                                                                    withLanguageC
                                                                                    ("en");
29        DetectSentimentResult detectSentimentResult = comprehendClient.detectSentiment(
            detectSentimentRequest);
30        System.out.println(detectSentimentResult);
31        System.out.println("End of DetectSentiment\n");
32        System.out.println( "Done" );
33    }
34 }
```

Detecting Sentiment Using the AWS SDK for Python (Boto)

The following Python program detects the sentiment of input text. You must specify the language of the input text.

```
1 import boto3
2 import json
3
4 comprehend = boto3.client(service_name='comprehend', region_name='region')
5
6 text = "It is raining today in Seattle"
7
8 print('Calling DetectSentiment')
9 print(json.dumps(comprehend.detect_sentiment(Text=text, LanguageCode='en'), sort_keys=True,
    indent=4))
10 print('End of DetectSentiment\n')
```

Using the Batch APIs

To send batches of up to 25 documents, you can use the Amazon Comprehend batch operations. Calling a batch operation is identical to calling the single document APIs for each document in the request. Using the batch APIs can result in better performance for you applications. For more information, see Batch Processing Documents.

- Batch Processing With the SDK for Java
- Batch Processing With the AWS CLI

Batch Processing With the SDK for Java

The following sample program shows how to use the [BatchDetectEntities APIrequestsBatchDetectEntities Inspects the text of a batch of documents for named entities and returns information about them. For more information about named entities, see Detecting Entities Request Syntax

```
1 {
2   "[LanguageCode](#comprehend-BatchDetectEntities-request-LanguageCode)": "string",
3   "[TextList](#comprehend-BatchDetectEntities-request-TextList)": [ "string" ]
4 }
5 ```   Request Parameters  For information about the parameters that are common to all actions,
      see [Common Parameters](CommonParameters.md)\. The request accepts the following data in
      JSON format\.
6
7 ** [LanguageCode](#API_BatchDetectEntities_RequestSyntax) **   <a name="comprehend-
      BatchDetectEntities-request-LanguageCode"></a>
8 The language of the input documents\. You can specify English \("en"\) or Spanish \("es"\)\. All
      documents must be in the same language\.
9 Type: String
10 Length Constraints: Minimum length of 1\.
11 Required: Yes
12
13 ** [TextList](#API_BatchDetectEntities_RequestSyntax) **   <a name="comprehend-
      BatchDetectEntities-request-TextList"></a>
14 A list containing the text of the input documents\. The list can contain a maximum of 25
      documents\. Each document must contain fewer than 5,000 bytes of UTF\-8 encoded characters\.
15 Type: Array of strings
16 Length Constraints: Minimum length of 1\.
17 Required: Yes    Response Syntax
```

{ "ErrorList": [{ "ErrorCode": "string", "ErrorMessage": "string", "Index": number }], "ResultList": [{ "Entities": [{ "BeginOffset": number, "EndOffset": number, "Score": number, "Text": "string", "Type": "string" }], "Index": number }] }

```
1
2 ** [ErrorList](#API_BatchDetectEntities_ResponseSyntax) **   <a name="comprehend-
      BatchDetectEntities-response-ErrorList"></a>
3 A list containing one [BatchItemError](API_BatchItemError.md) object for each document that
      contained an error\. The results are sorted in ascending order by the `Index` field and
      match the order of the documents in the input list\. If there are no errors in the batch,
      the `ErrorList` is empty\.
4 Type: Array of [BatchItemError](API_BatchItemError.md) objects
5
6 ** [ResultList](#API_BatchDetectEntities_ResponseSyntax) **   <a name="comprehend-
      BatchDetectEntities-response-ResultList"></a>
```

7 A list of [BatchDetectEntitiesItemResult](API_BatchDetectEntitiesItemResult.md) objects
   containing the results of the operation\. The results are sorted in ascending order by the `
   Index` field and match the order of the documents in the input list\. If all of the
   documents contain an error, the `ResultList` is empty\.

8 Type: Array of [BatchDetectEntitiesItemResult](API_BatchDetectEntitiesItemResult.md) objects
   Errors For information about the errors that are common to all actions, see [Common Errors
   ](CommonErrors.md)\.

9

10 **BatchSizeLimitExceededException**

11 The number of documents in the request exceeds the limit of 25\. Try your request again with
   fewer documents\.

12 HTTP Status Code: 400

13

14 **InternalServerException**

15 An internal server error occurred\. Retry your request\.

16 HTTP Status Code: 500

17

18 **InvalidRequestException**

19 The request is invalid\.

20 HTTP Status Code: 400

21

22 **TextSizeLimitExceededException**

23 The size of the input text exceeds the limit\. Use a smaller document\.

24 HTTP Status Code: 400

25

26 **UnsupportedLanguageException**

27 Amazon Comprehend can't process the language of the input text\. For all APIs except `
   DetectDominantLanguage`, Amazon Comprehend accepts only English or Spanish text\. For the `
   DetectDominantLanguage` API, Amazon Comprehend detects 100 languages\. For a list of
   languages, see [Detecting the Primary Language](how-languages.md)

28 HTTP Status Code: 400   See Also For more information about using this API in one of the
   language\-specific AWS SDKs, see the following: [AWS Command Line Interface](http://docs.
   aws.amazon.com/goto/aws-cli/comprehend-2017-11-27/BatchDetectEntities)   [AWS SDK for \.
   NET](http://docs.aws.amazon.com/goto/DotNetSDKV3/comprehend-2017-11-27/BatchDetectEntities)
        [AWS SDK for C\+\+](http://docs.aws.amazon.com/goto/SdkForCpp/comprehend-2017-11-27/
   BatchDetectEntities)   [AWS SDK for Go](http://docs.aws.amazon.com/goto/SdkForGoV1/
   comprehend-2017-11-27/BatchDetectEntities)   [AWS SDK for Java](http://docs.aws.amazon.com
   /goto/SdkForJava/comprehend-2017-11-27/BatchDetectEntities)   [AWS SDK for JavaScript](
   http://docs.aws.amazon.com/goto/AWSJavaScriptSDK/comprehend-2017-11-27/BatchDetectEntities)
        [AWS SDK for PHP V3](http://docs.aws.amazon.com/goto/SdkForPHPV3/comprehend-2017-11-27/
   BatchDetectEntities)   [AWS SDK for Python](http://docs.aws.amazon.com/goto/boto3/
   comprehend-2017-11-27/BatchDetectEntities)   [AWS SDK for Ruby V2](http://docs.aws.amazon.
   com/goto/SdkForRubyV2/comprehend-2017-11-27/BatchDetectEntities)   ](
   API_BatchDetectEntities.md) operation with the SDK for Java\. The response from the server
   contains a [BatchDetectEntitiesItemResult](API_BatchDetectEntitiesItemResult.md) object for
   each document that was successfully processed\. If there is an error processing a document
   there will be a record in the error list in the response\. The example gets each of the
   documents with an error and resends them\.

import com.amazonaws.auth.AWSStaticCredentialsProvider; import com.amazonaws.auth.DefaultAWSCreden-
tialsProviderChain;
import com.amazonaws.services.comprehend.AmazonComprehend; import com.amazonaws.services.compre-
hend.AmazonComprehendClientBuilder; import com.amazonaws.services.comprehend.model.BatchDetectEn-
titiesItemResult; import com.amazonaws.services.comprehend.model.BatchDetectEntitiesRequest; import
com.amazonaws.services.comprehend.model.BatchDetectEntitiesResult; import com.amazonaws.services.compre-

```
hend.model.BatchItemError;
public class App { public static void main( String[] args ) {
1    // Create credentials using a provider chain. For more information, see
2    // https://docs.aws.amazon.com/sdk-for-java/v1/developer-guide/credentials.html
3    AWSCredentialsProvider awsCreds = DefaultAWSCredentialsProviderChain.getInstance();
4
5    AmazonComprehend comprehendClient =
6        AmazonComprehendClientBuilder.standard()
7                                     .withCredentials(awsCreds)
8                                     .withRegion("region")
9                                     .build();
10
11   String[] textList = {"I love Seattle", "Today is Sunday", "Tomorrow is Monday", "I love
        Seattle"};
12
13   // Call detectEntities API
14   System.out.println("Calling BatchDetectEntities");
15   BatchDetectEntitiesRequest batchDetectEntitiesRequest = new BatchDetectEntitiesRequest().
        withTextList(textList)
16                                                                                    .withL
                                                                                      ("
                                                                                      en
                                                                                      ")
                                                                                      ;

17   BatchDetectEntitiesResult batchDetectEntitiesResult  = client.batchDetectEntities(
        batchDetectEntitiesRequest);
18
19   for(BatchDetectEntitiesItemResult item : batchDetectEntitiesResult.getResultList()) {
20       System.out.println(item);
21   }
22
23   // check if we need to retry failed requests
24   if (batchDetectEntitiesResult.getErrorList().size() != 0)
25   {
26       System.out.println("Retrying Failed Requests");
27       ArrayList<String> textToRetry = new ArrayList<String>();
28       for(BatchItemError errorItem : batchDetectEntitiesResult.getErrorList())
29       {
30           textToRetry.add(textList[errorItem.getIndex()]);
31       }
32
33       batchDetectEntitiesRequest = new BatchDetectEntitiesRequest().withTextList(textToRetry).
            withLanguageCode("en");
34       batchDetectEntitiesResult  = client.batchDetectEntities(batchDetectEntitiesRequest);
35
36       for(BatchDetectEntitiesItemResult item : batchDetectEntitiesResult.getResultList()) {
37           System.out.println(item);
38       }
39
40   }
41   System.out.println("End of DetectEntities");
42 }
```

}

Batch Processing With the AWS CLI

These examples show how to use the batch API operations using the AWS Command Line Interface\. All of the operations except `BatchDetectDominantLanguage` use the following JSON file called `process.json` as input\. For that operation the `LanguageCode` entity is not included\.

The third document in the JSON file \(`"$$$$$$$$"`\) will cause an error during batch processing \. It is included so that the operations will include a [BatchItemError](API_BatchItemError. md) in the response\.

{ "LanguageCode": "en", "TextList": ["I have been living in Seattle for almost 4 years", "It is raining today in Seattle", "$$$$$$$$"] }

The examples are formatted for Unix, Linux, and macOS\. For Windows, replace the backslash \(\\\) Unix continuation character at the end of each line with a caret \(^\)\.

+ [Detect the Dominant Language Using a Batch \(AWS CLI\)](#batch-dominant-language)
+ [Detect Entities Using a Batch \(AWS CLI\)](#batch-entities)
+ [Detect Key Phrases Using a Batch \(AWS CLI\)](#batch-key-phrase)
+ [Detect Sentiment Using a Batch \(AWS CLI\)](#batch-sentiment)

Detect the Dominant Language Using a Batch \(AWS CLI\)

The [BatchDetectDominantLanguage](API_BatchDetectDominantLanguage.md) operation determines the dominant language of each document in a batch\. For a list of the languages that Amazon Comprehend can detect, see [Detecting the Primary Language](how-languages.md)\. The following AWS CLI command calls the `BatchDetectDominantLanguage` operation\.

```
aws comprehend batch-detect-dominant-language
--endpoint endpoint
--region region
--cli-input-json file://path to input file/process.json
```

The following is the response from the `BatchDetectDominantLanguage` operation:

{ "ResultList": [{ "Index": 0, "Languages":[{ "LanguageCode":"en", "Score": 0.99 }] }, { "Index": 1 "Languages":[{ "LanguageCode":"en", "Score": 0.82 }] }], "ErrorList": [{ "Index": 2, "ErrorCode": "InternalServerException", "ErrorMessage": "Unexpected Server Error. Please try again." }] }

Detect Entities Using a Batch \(AWS CLI\)

Use the [BatchDetectEntities](API_BatchDetectEntities.md) operation to find the entities present in a batch of documents\. For more information about entities, see [Detecting Entities](how-entities.md)\. The following AWS CLI command calls the `BatchDetectEntities` operation\.

```
aws comprehend batch-detect-entities
--endpoint endpoint
--region region
--cli-input-json file://path to input file/process.json
```

1

2 ### Detect Key Phrases Using a Batch \(AWS CLI\)

3

4 The [BatchDetectKeyPhrases](API_BatchDetectKeyPhrases.md) operation returns the key noun phrases in a batch of documents\. The following AWS CLI command calls the ` BatchDetectKeyNounPhrases` operation\.

aws comprehend batch-detect-key-phrases --endpoint endpoint --region region --cli-input-json file://path to input file/process.json

1

2 ### Detect Sentiment Using a Batch \(AWS CLI\)

3

4 Detect the overall sentiment of a batch of documents using the [BatchDetectSentiment](API_BatchDetectSentiment.md) operation\. The following AWS CLI command calls the ` BatchDetectSentiment` operation\.

aws comprehend batch-detect-sentiment
--endpoint endpoint
--region region
--cli-input-json file://path to input file/process.json

1

2

3

4

5 # Authentication and Access Control for Amazon Comprehend

6

7 Access to Amazon Comprehend requires credentials that AWS can use to authenticate your requests \. Those credentials must have permissions to access Amazon Comprehend actions\. The following sections provide details on how you can use [AWS Identity and Access Management \(IAM\)](http://docs.aws.amazon.com/IAM/latest/UserGuide/introduction.html) and Amazon Comprehend to help secure your resources by controlling who can access them\.

8

9 + [Authentication](#authentication)

10

11 + [Access Control](#access-control)

12

13 ## Authentication

14

15 You can access AWS as any of the following types of identities:

16

17 + **AWS account root user** - When you first create an AWS account, you begin with a single sign \-in identity that has complete access to all AWS services and resources in the account\. This identity is called the AWS account *root user* and is accessed by signing in with the email address and password that you used to create the account\. We strongly recommend that you do not use the root user for your everyday tasks, even the administrative ones\. Instead , adhere to the [best practice of using the root user only to create your first IAM user](http://docs.aws.amazon.com/IAM/latest/UserGuide/best-practices.html#create-iam-users)\. Then securely lock away the root user credentials and use them to perform only a few account and service management tasks\.

18

19 + **IAM user** - An [IAM user](http://docs.aws.amazon.com/IAM/latest/UserGuide/id_users.html) is an identity within your AWS account that has specific custom permissions \(for example, permissions to create in Amazon Comprehend\)\. You can use an IAM user name and password to sign in to secure AWS webpages like the [AWS Management Console](https://console.aws.amazon.

com/), [AWS Discussion Forums](https://forums.aws.amazon.com/), or the [AWS Support Center](https://console.aws.amazon.com/support/home#/)\.

23 In addition to a user name and password, you can also generate [access keys](http://docs.aws. amazon.com/IAM/latest/UserGuide/id_credentials_access-keys.html) for each user\. You can use these keys when you access AWS services programmatically, either through [one of the several SDKs](https://aws.amazon.com/tools/) or by using the [AWS Command Line Interface \(CLI\)](https://aws.amazon.com/cli/)\. The SDK and CLI tools use the access keys to cryptographically sign your request\. If you 'dont use AWS tools, you must sign the request yourself\. Amazon Comprehend supports *Signature Version 4*, a protocol for authenticating inbound API requests\. For more information about authenticating requests, see [Signature Version 4 Signing Process](http://docs.aws.amazon.com/general/latest/gr/ signature-version-4.html) in the *AWS General Reference*\.

27 + **IAM role** - An [IAM role](http://docs.aws.amazon.com/IAM/latest/UserGuide/id_roles.html) is an IAM identity that you can create in your account that has specific permissions\. It is similar to an *IAM user*, but it is not associated with a specific person\. An IAM role enables you to obtain temporary access keys that can be used to access AWS services and resources\. IAM roles with temporary credentials are useful in the following situations:

31 + **Federated user access** - Instead of creating an IAM user, you can use existing user identities from AWS Directory Service, your enterprise user directory, or a web identity provider\. These are known as *federated users*\. AWS assigns a role to a federated user when access is requested through an [identity provider](http://docs.aws.amazon.com/IAM/ latest/UserGuide/id_roles_providers.html)\. For more information about federated users, see [Federated Users and Roles](http://docs.aws.amazon.com/IAM/latest/UserGuide/ introduction_access-management.html#intro-access-roles) in the *IAM User Guide*\.

35 + **AWS service access** - You can use an IAM role in your account to grant an AWS service permissions to access your 'accounts resources\. For example, you can create a role that allows Amazon Redshift to access an Amazon S3 bucket on your behalf and then load data from that bucket into an Amazon Redshift cluster\. For more information, see [Creating a Role to Delegate Permissions to an AWS Service](http://docs.aws.amazon.com/IAM/latest/ UserGuide/id_roles_create_for-service.html) in the *IAM User Guide*\.

39 + **Applications running on Amazon EC2** - You can use an IAM role to manage temporary credentials for applications that are running on an EC2 instance and making AWS API requests\. This is preferable to storing access keys within the EC2 instance\. To assign an AWS role to an EC2 instance and make it available to all of its applications, you create an instance profile that is attached to the instance\. An instance profile contains the role and enables programs that are running on the EC2 instance to get temporary credentials\. For more information, see [Using an IAM Role to Grant Permissions to Applications Running on Amazon EC2 Instances](http://docs.aws.amazon.com/IAM/latest/ UserGuide/id_roles_use_switch-role-ec2.html) in the *IAM User Guide*\.

40
Access Control

You must have valid credentials to authenticate your requests\. The credentials must have permissions to call an Amazon Comprehend action\.

The following sections describe how to manage permissions for Amazon Comprehend\. We recommend that you read the overview first\.

+ [Overview of Managing Access Permissions to Amazon Comprehend Resources](access-control-overview.md)

+ [Using Identity\-Based Polices \(IAM Policies\) for Amazon Comprehend](access-control-managing-permissions.md)

Overview of Managing Access Permissions to Amazon Comprehend Resources

Permissions to access an action are governed by permissions policies\. An account administrator can attach permissions policies to IAM identities \(that is, users, groups, and roles\) to manage access to actions\.

Note
An *account administrator* \(or administrator user\) is a user with administrator privileges\. For more information, see [IAM Best Practices](http://docs.aws.amazon.com/IAM/latest/UserGuide/best-practices.html) in the *IAM User Guide*\.

When granting permissions, you decide who is getting the permissions and the actions they get permissions for\.

+ [Managing Access to Actions](#access-control-manage-access-intro)
+ [Specifying Policy Elements: Actions, Effects, and Principals](#access-control-specify-comprehend-actions)
+ [Specifying Conditions in a Policy](#specifying-conditions)

Managing Access to Actions

A *permissions policy* describes who has access to what\. The following section explains the available options for creating permissions policies\.

Note
This section discusses using IAM in the context of Amazon Comprehend\. It doesn't provide detailed information about the IAM service\. For complete IAM documentation, see [What Is IAM?](http://docs.aws.amazon.com/IAM/latest/UserGuide/introduction.html) in the *IAM User Guide*\. For information about IAM policy syntax and descriptions, see [AWS IAM Policy Reference](http://docs.aws.amazon.com/IAM/latest/UserGuide/reference_policies.html) in the *IAM User Guide*\.

Policies attached to an IAM identity are referred to as *identity\-based* policies \(IAM polices\) and policies attached to a resource are referred to as *resource\-based* policies\.

Amazon Comprehend supports only identity\-based policies\.

76

77 ### Identity\-Based Policies \(IAM Policies\)

78

79 You can attach policies to IAM identities\. For example, you can do the following:

80

81 + **Attach a permissions policy to a user or a group in your account** - To grant a user or a group of users permissions to call and Amazon Comprehend action, you can attach a permissions policy to a user or group that the user belongs to\.

82

83 + **Attach a permissions policy to a role \(grant cross\-account permissions\)** - To grant cross\-account permissions, you can attach an identity\-based permissions policy to an IAM role\. For example, the administrator in Account A can create a role to grant cross\-account permissions to another AWS account \(for example, Account B\) or an AWS service as follows:

84

85   1. Account A administrator creates an IAM role and attaches a permissions policy to the role that grants permissions on resources in Account A\.

86

87   1. Account A administrator attaches a trust policy to the role identifying Account B as the principal who can assume the role\.

88

89   1. Account B administrator can then delegate permissions to assume the role to any users in Account B\. Doing this allows users in Account B to create or access resources in Account A\. If you want to grant an AWS service permissions to assume the role, the principal in the trust policy can also be an AWS service principal\.

90

91   For more information about using IAM to delegate permissions, see [Access Management](http://docs.aws.amazon.com/IAM/latest/UserGuide/access.html) in the *IAM User Guide*\.

92

93 For more information about using identity\-based policies with Amazon Comprehend, see [Using Identity\-Based Polices \(IAM Policies\) for Amazon Comprehend](access-control-managing-permissions.md)\. For more information about users, groups, roles, and permissions, see [Identities \(Users, Groups, and Roles\)](http://docs.aws.amazon.com/IAM/latest/UserGuide/id.html) in the *IAM User Guide*\.

94

95 ### Resource\-Based Policies

96

97 Other services, such as Lambda, support resource\-based permissions policies\. For example, you can attach a policy to an S3 bucket to manage access permissions to that bucket\. Amazon Comprehend doesn't support resource\-based policies\.

98

99 ## Specifying Policy Elements: Actions, Effects, and Principals

100

101 Amazon Comprehend defines a set of API operations \(see [Actions](API_Operations.md)\)\. To grant permissions for these API operations, Amazon Comprehend defines a set of actions that you can specify in a policy\.

102

103 The following are the most basic policy elements:

104

105 + **Resource** - In a policy, you use an Amazon Resource Name \(ARN\) to identify the resource to which the policy applies\. For Amazon Comprehend, the resource is always `"*"`\.

106

107 + **Action** - You use action keywords to identify operations that you want to allow or deny\. For example, depending on the specified `Effect`, `comprehend:DetectEntities` either allows or denies the user permissions to perform the Amazon Comprehend `DetectEntities` operation\.

108

109 + **Effect** - You specify the effect of the action that occurs when the user requests the specific -actionthis can be either allow or deny\. If you don't explicitly grant access to \(allow\) a resource, access is implicitly denied\. You can also explicitly deny access to a resource\. You might do this to make sure that a user cannot access the resource, even if a different policy grants access\.

110

111 + **Principal** - In identity\-based policies \(IAM policies\), the user that the policy is attached to is the implicit principal\.

112

113 To learn more about IAM policy syntax and descriptions, see [AWS IAM Policy Reference](http://docs.aws.amazon.com/IAM/latest/UserGuide/reference_policies.html) in the *IAM User Guide*\.

114

115 For a table showing all of the Amazon Comprehend API actions, see [Amazon Comprehend API Permissions: Actions, Resources, and Conditions Reference](comprehend-api-permissions-ref.md)\.

116

117 ## Specifying Conditions in a Policy

118

119 When you grant permissions, you use the IAM policy language to specify the conditions under which a policy should take effect\. For example, you might want a policy to be applied only after a specific date\. For more information about specifying conditions in a policy language, see [Condition](http://docs.aws.amazon.com/IAM/latest/UserGuide/reference_policies_elements.html#Condition) in the *IAM User Guide*\.

120

121 AWS provides a set of predefined condition keys for all AWS services that support IAM for access control\. For example, you can use the `aws:userid` condition key to require a specific AWS ID when requesting an action\. For more information and a complete list of AWS\-wide keys, see [Available Keys for Conditions](http://docs.aws.amazon.com/IAM/latest/UserGuide/reference_policies_elements.html#AvailableKeys) in the *IAM User Guide*\.

122

123 **Note**

124 Condition keys are case sensitive\.

125

126 Amazon Comprehend does not provide any additional condition keys\.

127

128

129

130

131 # Using Identity\-Based Polices \(IAM Policies\) for Amazon Comprehend

132

133 This topic provides examples of identity\-based policies that demonstrate how an account administrator can attach permissions policies to IAM identities \(that is, users, groups, and roles\) and thereby grant permissions to perform Amazon Comprehend actions\.

134

135 **Important**

136 Before you proceed, we recommend that you review [Overview of Managing Access Permissions to Amazon Comprehend Resources](access-control-overview.md)\.

137

138 The following is the permissions policy required to use the Amazon Comprehend document analysis

actions:

```
{ "Version": "2012-10-17", "Statement": [{ "Sid": "AllowDetectActions", "Effect": "Allow", "Action": [
"comprehend:DetectEntities", "comprehend:DetectKeyPhrases", "comprehend:DetectDominantLanguage", "com-
prehend:DetectSentiment" ],
"Resource": "*" } ] }
```

1

2 The policy has one statement that grants permission to use the `DetectEntities`, `
  DetectKeyPhrases`, `DetectDominantLanguage` and `DetectSentiment` actions\. A user with this
  policy would not be able to perform batch actions in your account\.

3

4 The policy doesn't specify the `Principal` element because you don't specify the principal who
  gets the permission in an identity\-based policy\. When you attach a policy to a user, the
  user is the implicit principal\. When you attach a permissions policy to an IAM role, the
  principal identified in the role's trust policy gets the permissions\.

5

6 For a table showing all of the Amazon Comprehend API actions and the resources that they apply
  to, see [Amazon Comprehend API Permissions: Actions, Resources, and Conditions Reference](
  comprehend-api-permissions-ref.md)\.

7

8 ## Permissions Required to Use the Amazon Comprehend Console<a name="auth-console-permissions
  "></a>

9

10 The permissions reference table lists the Amazon Comprehend API operations and shows the
  required permissions for each operation\. For more information, about Amazon Comprehend API
  permissions, see [Amazon Comprehend API Permissions: Actions, Resources, and Conditions
  Reference](comprehend-api-permissions-ref.md)\.

11

12 To use the Amazon Comprehend console, you need to grant permissions for the actions shown in the
  following policy:

```
{ "Version": "2012-10-17", "Statement": [ { "Action": [ "comprehend:", "iam:ListRoles", "iam:GetRole",
"s3:ListAllMyBuckets", "s3:ListBucket", "s3:GetBucketLocation" ], "Effect": "Allow", "Resource": "" } ] }
```

1

2 The Amazon Comprehend console needs these additional permissions for the following reasons:

3

4 + `iam` permissions to list the available IAM roles for your account\.

5

6 + `s3` permissions to access the Amazon S3 buckets and objects that contain the data for topic
  modeling\.

7

8 When you create a topic modeling job using the console, you have the option to have the console
  create an IAM role for your job\. To create an IAM role, users must be granted the following
  additional permissions to create IAM roles and policies, and to attach policies to roles:

```
{ "Version": "2012-10-17", "Statement": [ { "Action": [ "iam:CreateRole", "iam:CreatePolicy", "iam:AttachRole-
Policy", "iam:PassRole" ], "Effect": "Allow", "Resource": "*" } ] }
```

1

2 The Amazon Comprehend console needs these additional permissions for the following reasons:

3

4 + `iam` permissions to create roles and policies and to attach roles and polices\. The `iam:
  PassRole` action enables the console to pass the role to Amazon Comprehend\.

5

6 ## AWS Managed \(Predefined\) Policies for Amazon Comprehend

7

8 AWS addresses many common use cases by providing standalone IAM policies that are created and administered by AWS\. These AWS managed policies grant necessary permissions for common use cases so that you can avoid having to investigate what permissions are needed\. For more information, see [AWS Managed Policies](http://docs.aws.amazon.com/IAM/latest/UserGuide/access_policies_managed-vs-inline.html#aws-managed-policies) in the *IAM User Guide*\.

9

10 The following AWS managed policies, which you can attach to users in your account, are specific to Amazon Comprehend:

11

12 + **ComprehendFullAccess** - Grants full access to Amazon Comprehend resources including running topic modeling jobs\. Includes permission to list and get IAM roles\.

13

14 + **ComprehendReadOnly** - Grants permission to run all Amazon Comprehend actions except `StartTopicsDetectionJob`\.

15

16 You need to apply the following additional policy to any user that will use Amazon Comprehend:

{ "Version": "2012-10-17", "Statement": [{ "Action": ["iam:PassRole"], "Effect": "Allow", "Resource": "*" }] }

1

2 You can review the managed permissions policies by signing in to the IAM console and searching for specific policies there\.

3

4 These policies work when you are using AWS SDKs or the AWS CLI\.

5

6 You can also create your own custom IAM policies to allow permissions for Amazon Comprehend actions and resources\. You can attach these custom policies to the IAM users or groups that require those permissions\.

7

8 ## Role\-Based Permissions Required for Topic Detection

9

10 To use the Amazon Comprehend topic detection operations, you must grant Amazon Comprehend access to the Amazon S3 bucket that contains your document collection\. You do this by creating a data access role in your account to trust the Amazon Comprehend service principal\. For more information about creating a role, see [Creating a Role to Delegate Permissions to an AWS Service](http://docs.aws.amazon.com/IAM/latest/UserGuide/id_roles_create_for-service.html) in the *AWS Identity and Access Management User Guide*\.

11

12 The following is the role's trust policy:

{ "Version": "2012-10-17", "Statement": [{ "Effect": "Allow", "Principal": { "Service": "comprehend.amazon-aws.com" }, "Action": "sts:AssumeRole" }] }

1

2 After you have created the role, you must create an access policy for that role\. The should grant the Amazon S3 `GetObject` and `ListBucket` permissions to the Amazon S3 bucket that contains your input data, and the Amazon S3 `PutObject` permission to your Amazon S3 output data bucket\.

3

4 The following example access policy contains those permissions\.

{ "Version": "2012-10-17", "Statement": [{ "Action": ["s3:GetObject"], "Resource": ["arn:aws:s3:::input bucket/"], "Effect": "Allow" }, { "Action": ["s3:ListBucket"], "Resource": ["arn:aws:s3:::input bucket"], "Effect": "Allow" }, { "Action": ["s3:PutObject"], "Resource": ["arn:aws:s3:::output bucket/"], "Effect": "Allow" }] }

1
2 ## Customer Managed Policy Examples
3
4 In this section, you can find example user policies that grant permissions for various Amazon Comprehend actions\. These policies work when you are using AWS SDKs or the AWS CLI\. When you are using the console, you need to grant permissions to all the Amazon Comprehend APIs\. This is discussed in [Permissions Required to Use the Amazon Comprehend Console](#auth-console-permissions)\.
5
6 **Note**
7 All examples use the us\-east\-2 region and contain fictitious account IDs\.
8
9 **Examples**
10
11 ### Example 1: Allow All Amazon Comprehend Actions
12
13 After you sign up for AWS, you create an administrator user to manage your account, including creating users and managing their permissions\.
14
15 You might choose to create a user who has permissions for all Amazon Comprehend actions \(think of this user as a service\-specific administrator\) for working with Amazon Comprehend\. You can attach the following permissions policy to this user\.

{ "Version": "2012-10-17", "Statement": [{ "Sid": "AllowAllComprehendActions", "Effect": "Allow", "Action": ["comprehend:"], "Resource": "" }] }

1
2 ### Example 2: Allow Topic Modeling Actions
3
4 The following permissions policy grants user permissions to perform the Amazon Comprehend topic modeling operations\.

{ "Version": "2012-10-17", "Statement": [{ "Sid": "AllowTopicModelingActions", "Effect": "Allow", "Action": ["comprehend:DescribeTopicsDetectionJob", "comprehend:ListTopicsDetectionJobs", "comprehend:StartTopicsDetectionJob",],
"Resource": "*"] }] }

1
2
3
4
5 # Amazon Comprehend API Permissions: Actions, Resources, and Conditions Reference
6
7 Use the following table as a reference when setting up [Access Control](auth-and-access-control.md#access-control) and writing a permissions policy that you can attach to an IAM identity \(an identity\-based policy\)\. The list includes each Amazon Comprehend API operation, the corresponding action for which you can grant permissions to perform the action, and the AWS resource for which you can grant the permissions\. You specify the actions in the policy's `Action` field, and you specify the resource value in the policy's `Resource` field\.
8

9 To express conditions, you can use AWS\-wide condition keys in your Amazon Comprehend policies\. For a complete list of AWS\-wide keys, see [Available Keys](http://docs.aws.amazon.com/IAM/latest/UserGuide/reference_policies_elements.html#AvailableKeys) in the *IAM User Guide*\.

10

11 **Note**

12 To specify an action, use the `comprehend:` prefix followed by the API operation name, for example, `comprehend:DetectEntities`\.

13

14 If you see an expand arrow \(****\) in the upper\-right corner of the table, you can open the table in a new window\. To close the window, choose the close button \(**X**\) in the lower \-right corner\.

15

16

17 **Amazon Comprehend API and Required Permissions for Actions**

18

19 | Amazon Comprehend API Operations | Required Permissions \(API Actions\) | Resources |

20 | --- | --- | --- |

21 | [BatchDetectDominantLanguage](API_BatchDetectDominantLanguage.md) | comprehend:BatchDetectDominantLanguage | * |

22 | [BatchDetectEntities](API_BatchDetectEntities.md) | comprehend:BatchDetectEntities | * |

23 | [BatchDetectKeyPhrases](API_BatchDetectKeyPhrases.md) | comprehend:BatchDetectKeyPhrases | * |

24 | [BatchDetectSentiment](API_BatchDetectSentiment.md) | comprehend:BatchDetectSentiment | * |

25 | [DescribeTopicsDetectionJob](API_DescribeTopicsDetectionJob.md) | comprehend:DescribeTopicsDetectionJob | * |

26 | [DetectDominantLanguage](API_DetectDominantLanguage.md) | comprehend:DetectDominantLanguage | * |

27 | [DetectEntities](API_DetectEntities.md) | comprehend:DetectEntities | * |

28 | [DetectKeyPhrases](API_DetectKeyPhrases.md) | comprehend:DetectKeyPhrases | * |

29 | [DetectSentiment](API_DetectSentiment.md) | comprehend:DetectSentiment | * |

30 | [ListTopicsDetectionJobs](API_ListTopicsDetectionJobs.md) | comprehend:ListTopicsDectectionJobs | * |

31 | [StartTopicsDetectionJob](API_StartTopicsDetectionJob.md) | comprehend:StartTopicsDetectionJob | * |

32

33

34

35

36 # Guidelines and Limits

37

38 Keep in mind the following information when using Amazon Comprehend\.

39

40 ## Supported Regions

41

42 For a list of AWS Regions where Amazon Comprehend is availabe, see [AWS Regions and Endpoints](https://docs.aws.amazon.com/general/latest/gr/rande.html#comprehend_region) in the *Amazon Web Services General Reference*\.

43

44 ## Throttling

45

46 For information about throttling for Amazon Comprehend and to request a limit increase, see [Amazon Comprehend Limits](https://docs.aws.amazon.com/general/latest/gr/aws_service_limits.html#limits_amazon_comprehend) in the *Amazon Web Services General Reference*\.

47

48 You may be able to avoid throttling by using the batch operations instead of the single transaction operations\. For more information, see [Batch Operations](#limits-batch)\.

49

50 ## Overall Limits

51

52 All operations except topic modeling operations have the following limits:

53

54

55 | Description | Limit |
56 | --- | --- |
57 | Character encoding | UTF\-8 |
58 | Document size \(UTF\-8 characters\) | 5,000 bytes |

59

60 ## Batch Operations

61

62 The [BatchDetectDominantLanguage](API_BatchDetectDominantLanguage.md), [BatchDetectEntities](API_BatchDetectEntities.md), [BatchDetectKeyPhrases](API_BatchDetectKeyPhrases.md), and [BatchDetectSentiment](API_BatchDetectSentiment.md) operations have the following limits:

63

64

65 | Description | Limit |
66 | --- | --- |
67 | Documents per request | 25 |

68

69 If you plan to send more than 20 requests per second, you should consider using the batch operations\. Batch operations enable you to send more documents in each request which may result in higher throughput\. For example, when you use the `DetectDominantLanguage` operation, you can send up to 20 documents per second\. However, if you use the `BatchRequestDominantLanguage` operation, you can send up to 250 documents per second, but processing speed may be lower\. For more information about throttling limits see [Amazon Comprehend Limits](https://docs.aws.amazon.com/general/latest/gr/aws_service_limits.html#limits_amazon_comprehend) in the *Amazon Web Services General Reference*\. For more information about using the batch APIs, see [Batch Processing Documents](how-batch.md)\.

70

71 ## Language Detection

72

73 The [BatchDetectDominantLanguage](API_BatchDetectDominantLanguage.md) and [DetectDominantLanguage](API_DetectDominantLanguage.md) operations have the following limitations:

74

75 + They don't support phonetic language detection\. For example, they will not detect "arigato" as Japanese nor "nihao" as Chinese\.

76

77 + They may have trouble distinguishing close language pairs, such as Indonesian and Malay; or Bosnian, Croation, and Serbian\.

78

79 + For best results the input text should be at least 20 characters long\.

80

81 ## Topic Modeling

82

83 Topic detection jobs created with the [StartTopicsDetectionJob](API_StartTopicsDetectionJob.md) operation have the following limits:

84

85

Description	Limit
Character encoding	UTF\-8
Maximum number of topics to return	100
Total size of all files in request	1 Gb
Maximum file size for one file	2 Mb
Maximum number of files, one document per file	50,000
Maximum number of lines, one document per line	1,000,000

For best results, you should include at least 1,000 input documents\.

API Reference

This section provides documentation for the Amazon Comprehend API operations\.

Actions

The following actions are supported:

+ [BatchDetectDominantLanguage](API_BatchDetectDominantLanguage.md)

+ [BatchDetectEntities](API_BatchDetectEntities.md)

+ [BatchDetectKeyPhrases](API_BatchDetectKeyPhrases.md)

+ [BatchDetectSentiment](API_BatchDetectSentiment.md)

+ [DescribeTopicsDetectionJob](API_DescribeTopicsDetectionJob.md)

+ [DetectDominantLanguage](API_DetectDominantLanguage.md)

+ [DetectEntities](API_DetectEntities.md)

+ [DetectKeyPhrases](API_DetectKeyPhrases.md)

+ [DetectSentiment](API_DetectSentiment.md)

+ [ListTopicsDetectionJobs](API_ListTopicsDetectionJobs.md)

+ [StartTopicsDetectionJob](API_StartTopicsDetectionJob.md)

BatchDetectDominantLanguage

Determines the dominant language of the input text for a batch of documents\. For a list of languages that Amazon Comprehend can detect, see [Amazon Comprehend Supported Languages](

http://docs.aws.amazon.com/comprehend/latest/dg/how-languages.html)\.

139

140 ## Request Syntax

{ "TextList": ["string"] }

1

2 ## Request Parameters

3

4 For information about the parameters that are common to all actions, see [Common Parameters](
   CommonParameters.md)\.

5

6 The request accepts the following data in JSON format\.

7

8 ** [TextList](#API_BatchDetectDominantLanguage_RequestSyntax) **   <a name="comprehend-
   BatchDetectDominantLanguage-request-TextList"></a>

9 A list containing the text of the input documents\. The list can contain a maximum of 25
   documents\. Each document should contain at least 20 characters and must contain fewer than
   5,000 bytes of UTF\-8 encoded characters\.

10 Type: Array of strings

11 Length Constraints: Minimum length of 1\.

12 Required: Yes

13

14 ## Response Syntax

{ "ErrorList": [{ "ErrorCode": "string", "ErrorMessage": "string", "Index": number }], "ResultList": [{
"Index": number, "Languages": [{ "LanguageCode": "string", "Score": number }] }] }

1

2 ## Response Elements

3

4 If the action is successful, the service sends back an HTTP 200 response\.

5

6 The following data is returned in JSON format by the service\.

7

8 ** [ErrorList](#API_BatchDetectDominantLanguage_ResponseSyntax) **   <a name="comprehend-
   BatchDetectDominantLanguage-response-ErrorList"></a>

9 A list containing one [BatchItemError](API_BatchItemError.md) object for each document that
   contained an error\. The results are sorted in ascending order by the `Index` field and
   match the order of the documents in the input list\. If there are no errors in the batch,
   the `ErrorList` is empty\.

10 Type: Array of [BatchItemError](API_BatchItemError.md) objects

11

12 ** [ResultList](#API_BatchDetectDominantLanguage_ResponseSyntax) **   <a name="comprehend-
   BatchDetectDominantLanguage-response-ResultList"></a>

13 A list of [BatchDetectDominantLanguageItemResult](API_BatchDetectDominantLanguageItemResult.md)
   objects containing the results of the operation\. The results are sorted in ascending order
   by the `Index` field and match the order of the documents in the input list\. If all of the
   documents contain an error, the `ResultList` is empty\.

14 Type: Array of [BatchDetectDominantLanguageItemResult](API_BatchDetectDominantLanguageItemResult
   .md) objects

15

16 ## Errors

17

18 For information about the errors that are common to all actions, see [Common Errors](
   CommonErrors.md)\.

BatchSizeLimitExceededException
The number of documents in the request exceeds the limit of 25\. Try your request again with
    fewer documents\.
HTTP Status Code: 400

InternalServerException
An internal server error occurred\. Retry your request\.
HTTP Status Code: 500

InvalidRequestException
The request is invalid\.
HTTP Status Code: 400

TextSizeLimitExceededException
The size of the input text exceeds the limit\. Use a smaller document\.
HTTP Status Code: 400

See Also

For more information about using this API in one of the language\-specific AWS SDKs, see the
    following:

+ [AWS Command Line Interface](http://docs.aws.amazon.com/goto/aws-cli/comprehend-2017-11-27/
    BatchDetectDominantLanguage)

+ [AWS SDK for \.NET](http://docs.aws.amazon.com/goto/DotNetSDKV3/comprehend-2017-11-27/
    BatchDetectDominantLanguage)

+ [AWS SDK for C\+\+](http://docs.aws.amazon.com/goto/SdkForCpp/comprehend-2017-11-27/
    BatchDetectDominantLanguage)

+ [AWS SDK for Go](http://docs.aws.amazon.com/goto/SdkForGoV1/comprehend-2017-11-27/
    BatchDetectDominantLanguage)

+ [AWS SDK for Java](http://docs.aws.amazon.com/goto/SdkForJava/comprehend-2017-11-27/
    BatchDetectDominantLanguage)

+ [AWS SDK for JavaScript](http://docs.aws.amazon.com/goto/AWSJavaScriptSDK/comprehend
    -2017-11-27/BatchDetectDominantLanguage)

+ [AWS SDK for PHP V3](http://docs.aws.amazon.com/goto/SdkForPHPV3/comprehend-2017-11-27/
    BatchDetectDominantLanguage)

+ [AWS SDK for Python](http://docs.aws.amazon.com/goto/boto3/comprehend-2017-11-27/
    BatchDetectDominantLanguage)

+ [AWS SDK for Ruby V2](http://docs.aws.amazon.com/goto/SdkForRubyV2/comprehend-2017-11-27/
    BatchDetectDominantLanguage)

BatchDetectEntities

62

63 Inspects the text of a batch of documents for named entities and returns information about them \. For more information about named entities, see [Detecting Entities](how-entities.md)

64

65 ## Request Syntax

{ "LanguageCode": "string", "TextList": ["string"] }

1

2 ## Request Parameters

3

4 For information about the parameters that are common to all actions, see [Common Parameters](CommonParameters.md)\.

5

6 The request accepts the following data in JSON format\.

7

8 ** [LanguageCode](#API_BatchDetectEntities_RequestSyntax) **

9 The language of the input documents\. You can specify English \("en"\) or Spanish \("es"\)\. All documents must be in the same language\.

10 Type: String

11 Length Constraints: Minimum length of 1\.

12 Required: Yes

13

14 ** [TextList](#API_BatchDetectEntities_RequestSyntax) **

15 A list containing the text of the input documents\. The list can contain a maximum of 25 documents\. Each document must contain fewer than 5,000 bytes of UTF\-8 encoded characters\.

16 Type: Array of strings

17 Length Constraints: Minimum length of 1\.

18 Required: Yes

19

20 ## Response Syntax

{ "ErrorList": [{ "ErrorCode": "string", "ErrorMessage": "string", "Index": number }], "ResultList": [{ "Entities": [{ "BeginOffset": number, "EndOffset": number, "Score": number, "Text": "string", "Type": "string" }], "Index": number }] }

1

2 ## Response Elements

3

4 If the action is successful, the service sends back an HTTP 200 response\.

5

6 The following data is returned in JSON format by the service\.

7

8 ** [ErrorList](#API_BatchDetectEntities_ResponseSyntax) **

9 A list containing one [BatchItemError](API_BatchItemError.md) object for each document that contained an error\. The results are sorted in ascending order by the `Index` field and match the order of the documents in the input list\. If there are no errors in the batch, the `ErrorList` is empty\.

10 Type: Array of [BatchItemError](API_BatchItemError.md) objects

11

12 ** [ResultList](#API_BatchDetectEntities_ResponseSyntax) **

13 A list of [BatchDetectEntitiesItemResult](API_BatchDetectEntitiesItemResult.md) objects
    containing the results of the operation\. The results are sorted in ascending order by the `
    Index` field and match the order of the documents in the input list\. If all of the
    documents contain an error, the `ResultList` is empty\.
14 Type: Array of [BatchDetectEntitiesItemResult](API_BatchDetectEntitiesItemResult.md) objects
15
16 ## Errors
17
18 For information about the errors that are common to all actions, see [Common Errors](
    CommonErrors.md)\.
19
20 **BatchSizeLimitExceededException**
21 The number of documents in the request exceeds the limit of 25\. Try your request again with
    fewer documents\.
22 HTTP Status Code: 400
23
24 **InternalServerException**
25 An internal server error occurred\. Retry your request\.
26 HTTP Status Code: 500
27
28 **InvalidRequestException**
29 The request is invalid\.
30 HTTP Status Code: 400
31
32 **TextSizeLimitExceededException**
33 The size of the input text exceeds the limit\. Use a smaller document\.
34 HTTP Status Code: 400
35
36 **UnsupportedLanguageException**
37 Amazon Comprehend can't process the language of the input text\. For all APIs except `
    DetectDominantLanguage`, Amazon Comprehend accepts only English or Spanish text\. For the `
    DetectDominantLanguage` API, Amazon Comprehend detects 100 languages\. For a list of
    languages, see [Detecting the Primary Language](how-languages.md)
38 HTTP Status Code: 400
39
40 ## See Also
41
42 For more information about using this API in one of the language\-specific AWS SDKs, see the
    following:
43
44 +   [AWS Command Line Interface](http://docs.aws.amazon.com/goto/aws-cli/comprehend-2017-11-27/
    BatchDetectEntities)
45
46 +   [AWS SDK for \.NET](http://docs.aws.amazon.com/goto/DotNetSDKV3/comprehend-2017-11-27/
    BatchDetectEntities)
47
48 +   [AWS SDK for C\+\+](http://docs.aws.amazon.com/goto/SdkForCpp/comprehend-2017-11-27/
    BatchDetectEntities)
49
50 +   [AWS SDK for Go](http://docs.aws.amazon.com/goto/SdkForGoV1/comprehend-2017-11-27/
    BatchDetectEntities)
51
52 +   [AWS SDK for Java](http://docs.aws.amazon.com/goto/SdkForJava/comprehend-2017-11-27/
    BatchDetectEntities)

53

54 + [AWS SDK for JavaScript](http://docs.aws.amazon.com/goto/AWSJavaScriptSDK/comprehend
-2017-11-27/BatchDetectEntities)

55

56 + [AWS SDK for PHP V3](http://docs.aws.amazon.com/goto/SdkForPHPV3/comprehend-2017-11-27/
BatchDetectEntities)

57

58 + [AWS SDK for Python](http://docs.aws.amazon.com/goto/boto3/comprehend-2017-11-27/
BatchDetectEntities)

59

60 + [AWS SDK for Ruby V2](http://docs.aws.amazon.com/goto/SdkForRubyV2/comprehend-2017-11-27/
BatchDetectEntities)

61

62

63

64

65 # BatchDetectKeyPhrases

66

67 Detects the key noun phrases found in a batch of documents\.

68

69 ## Request Syntax

{ "LanguageCode": "string", "TextList": ["string"] }

1

2 ## Request Parameters

3

4 For information about the parameters that are common to all actions, see [Common Parameters](
CommonParameters.md)\.

5

6 The request accepts the following data in JSON format\.

7

8 ** [LanguageCode](#API_BatchDetectKeyPhrases_RequestSyntax) **   <a name="comprehend-
BatchDetectKeyPhrases-request-LanguageCode"></a>

9 The language of the input documents\. You can specify English \("en"\) or Spanish \("es"\)\. All
documents must be in the same language\.

10 Type: String

11 Length Constraints: Minimum length of 1\.

12 Required: Yes

13

14 ** [TextList](#API_BatchDetectKeyPhrases_RequestSyntax) **   <a name="comprehend-
BatchDetectKeyPhrases-request-TextList"></a>

15 A list containing the text of the input documents\. The list can contain a maximum of 25
documents\. Each document must contain fewer that 5,000 bytes of UTF\-8 encoded characters\.

16 Type: Array of strings

17 Length Constraints: Minimum length of 1\.

18 Required: Yes

19

20 ## Response Syntax

{ "ErrorList": [{ "ErrorCode": "string", "ErrorMessage": "string", "Index": number }], "ResultList": [{
"Index": number, "KeyPhrases": [{ "BeginOffset": number, "EndOffset": number, "Score": number, "Text":
"string" }] }] }

1

2 ## Response Elements

3

4 If the action is successful, the service sends back an HTTP 200 response\.

5

6 The following data is returned in JSON format by the service\.

7

8 ** [ErrorList](#API_BatchDetectKeyPhrases_ResponseSyntax) **

9 A list containing one [BatchItemError](API_BatchItemError.md) object for each document that contained an error\. The results are sorted in ascending order by the `Index` field and match the order of the documents in the input list\. If there are no errors in the batch, the `ErrorList` is empty\.

10 Type: Array of [BatchItemError](API_BatchItemError.md) objects

11

12 ** [ResultList](#API_BatchDetectKeyPhrases_ResponseSyntax) **

13 A list of [BatchDetectKeyPhrasesItemResult](API_BatchDetectKeyPhrasesItemResult.md) objects containing the results of the operation\. The results are sorted in ascending order by the `Index` field and match the order of the documents in the input list\. If all of the documents contain an error, the `ResultList` is empty\.

14 Type: Array of [BatchDetectKeyPhrasesItemResult](API_BatchDetectKeyPhrasesItemResult.md) objects

15

16 ## Errors

17

18 For information about the errors that are common to all actions, see [Common Errors](CommonErrors.md)\.

19

20 **BatchSizeLimitExceededException**

21 The number of documents in the request exceeds the limit of 25\. Try your request again with fewer documents\.

22 HTTP Status Code: 400

23

24 **InternalServerException**

25 An internal server error occurred\. Retry your request\.

26 HTTP Status Code: 500

27

28 **InvalidRequestException**

29 The request is invalid\.

30 HTTP Status Code: 400

31

32 **TextSizeLimitExceededException**

33 The size of the input text exceeds the limit\. Use a smaller document\.

34 HTTP Status Code: 400

35

36 **UnsupportedLanguageException**

37 Amazon Comprehend can't process the language of the input text\. For all APIs except `DetectDominantLanguage`, Amazon Comprehend accepts only English or Spanish text\. For the `DetectDominantLanguage` API, Amazon Comprehend detects 100 languages\. For a list of languages, see [Detecting the Primary Language](how-languages.md)

38 HTTP Status Code: 400

39

40 ## See Also

41

42 For more information about using this API in one of the language\-specific AWS SDKs, see the following:

43

44 + [AWS Command Line Interface](http://docs.aws.amazon.com/goto/aws-cli/comprehend-2017-11-27/
BatchDetectKeyPhrases)

45

46 + [AWS SDK for \.NET](http://docs.aws.amazon.com/goto/DotNetSDKV3/comprehend-2017-11-27/
BatchDetectKeyPhrases)

47

48 + [AWS SDK for C\+\+](http://docs.aws.amazon.com/goto/SdkForCpp/comprehend-2017-11-27/
BatchDetectKeyPhrases)

49

50 + [AWS SDK for Go](http://docs.aws.amazon.com/goto/SdkForGoV1/comprehend-2017-11-27/
BatchDetectKeyPhrases)

51

52 + [AWS SDK for Java](http://docs.aws.amazon.com/goto/SdkForJava/comprehend-2017-11-27/
BatchDetectKeyPhrases)

53

54 + [AWS SDK for JavaScript](http://docs.aws.amazon.com/goto/AWSJavaScriptSDK/comprehend
-2017-11-27/BatchDetectKeyPhrases)

55

56 + [AWS SDK for PHP V3](http://docs.aws.amazon.com/goto/SdkForPHPV3/comprehend-2017-11-27/
BatchDetectKeyPhrases)

57

58 + [AWS SDK for Python](http://docs.aws.amazon.com/goto/boto3/comprehend-2017-11-27/
BatchDetectKeyPhrases)

59

60 + [AWS SDK for Ruby V2](http://docs.aws.amazon.com/goto/SdkForRubyV2/comprehend-2017-11-27/
BatchDetectKeyPhrases)

61

62

63

64

65 # BatchDetectSentiment

66

67 Inspects a batch of documents and returns an inference of the prevailing sentiment, `POSITIVE`,
`NEUTRAL`, `MIXED`, or `NEGATIVE`, in each one\.

68

69 ## Request Syntax

  { "LanguageCode": "string", "TextList": ["string"] }

1

2 ## Request Parameters

3

4 For information about the parameters that are common to all actions, see [Common Parameters](
CommonParameters.md)\.

5

6 The request accepts the following data in JSON format\.

7

8 ** [LanguageCode](#API_BatchDetectSentiment_RequestSyntax) **   <a name="comprehend-
BatchDetectSentiment-request-LanguageCode"></a>

9 The language of the input documents\. You can specify English \("en"\) or Spanish \("es"\)\. All
documents must be in the same language\.

10 Type: String

11 Length Constraints: Minimum length of 1\.

12 Required: Yes

13

14 ** [TextList](#API_BatchDetectSentiment_RequestSyntax) **

15 A list containing the text of the input documents\. The list can contain a maximum of 25 documents\. Each document must contain fewer that 5,000 bytes of UTF\-8 encoded characters\.

16 Type: Array of strings

17 Length Constraints: Minimum length of 1\.

18 Required: Yes

19

20 ## Response Syntax

{ "ErrorList": [{ "ErrorCode": "string", "ErrorMessage": "string", "Index": number }], "ResultList": [{ "Index": number, "Sentiment": "string", "SentimentScore": { "Mixed": number, "Negative": number, "Neutral": number, "Positive": number } }] }

1

2 ## Response Elements

3

4 If the action is successful, the service sends back an HTTP 200 response\.

5

6 The following data is returned in JSON format by the service\.

7

8 ** [ErrorList](#API_BatchDetectSentiment_ResponseSyntax) **

9 A list containing one [BatchItemError](API_BatchItemError.md) object for each document that contained an error\. The results are sorted in ascending order by the `Index` field and match the order of the documents in the input list\. If there are no errors in the batch, the `ErrorList` is empty\.

10 Type: Array of [BatchItemError](API_BatchItemError.md) objects

11

12 ** [ResultList](#API_BatchDetectSentiment_ResponseSyntax) **

13 A list of [BatchDetectSentimentItemResult](API_BatchDetectSentimentItemResult.md) objects containing the results of the operation\. The results are sorted in ascending order by the `Index` field and match the order of the documents in the input list\. If all of the documents contain an error, the `ResultList` is empty\.

14 Type: Array of [BatchDetectSentimentItemResult](API_BatchDetectSentimentItemResult.md) objects

15

16 ## Errors

17

18 For information about the errors that are common to all actions, see [Common Errors](CommonErrors.md)\.

19

20 **BatchSizeLimitExceededException**

21 The number of documents in the request exceeds the limit of 25\. Try your request again with fewer documents\.

22 HTTP Status Code: 400

23

24 **InternalServerException**

25 An internal server error occurred\. Retry your request\.

26 HTTP Status Code: 500

27

28 **InvalidRequestException**

29 The request is invalid\.

30 HTTP Status Code: 400

31

32 **TextSizeLimitExceededException**
33 The size of the input text exceeds the limit\. Use a smaller document\.
34 HTTP Status Code: 400

35

36 **UnsupportedLanguageException**
37 Amazon Comprehend can't process the language of the input text\. For all APIs except `DetectDominantLanguage`, Amazon Comprehend accepts only English or Spanish text\. For the `DetectDominantLanguage` API, Amazon Comprehend detects 100 languages\. For a list of languages, see [Detecting the Primary Language](how-languages.md)
38 HTTP Status Code: 400

39

40 ## See Also

41

42 For more information about using this API in one of the language\-specific AWS SDKs, see the following:

43

44 + [AWS Command Line Interface](http://docs.aws.amazon.com/goto/aws-cli/comprehend-2017-11-27/BatchDetectSentiment)

45

46 + [AWS SDK for \.NET](http://docs.aws.amazon.com/goto/DotNetSDKV3/comprehend-2017-11-27/BatchDetectSentiment)

47

48 + [AWS SDK for C\+\+](http://docs.aws.amazon.com/goto/SdkForCpp/comprehend-2017-11-27/BatchDetectSentiment)

49

50 + [AWS SDK for Go](http://docs.aws.amazon.com/goto/SdkForGoV1/comprehend-2017-11-27/BatchDetectSentiment)

51

52 + [AWS SDK for Java](http://docs.aws.amazon.com/goto/SdkForJava/comprehend-2017-11-27/BatchDetectSentiment)

53

54 + [AWS SDK for JavaScript](http://docs.aws.amazon.com/goto/AWSJavaScriptSDK/comprehend-2017-11-27/BatchDetectSentiment)

55

56 + [AWS SDK for PHP V3](http://docs.aws.amazon.com/goto/SdkForPHPV3/comprehend-2017-11-27/BatchDetectSentiment)

57

58 + [AWS SDK for Python](http://docs.aws.amazon.com/goto/boto3/comprehend-2017-11-27/BatchDetectSentiment)

59

60 + [AWS SDK for Ruby V2](http://docs.aws.amazon.com/goto/SdkForRubyV2/comprehend-2017-11-27/BatchDetectSentiment)

61

62

63

64

65 # DescribeTopicsDetectionJob

66

67 Gets the properties associated with a topic detection job\. Use this operation to get the status of a detection job\.

68

69 ## Request Syntax

```
{ "JobId": "string" }
```

Request Parameters

For information about the parameters that are common to all actions, see [Common Parameters](CommonParameters.md)\.

The request accepts the following data in JSON format\.

** [JobId](#API_DescribeTopicsDetectionJob_RequestSyntax) **
The identifier assigned by the user to the detection job\.
Type: String
Length Constraints: Minimum length of 1\. Maximum length of 32\.
Required: Yes

Response Syntax

{ "TopicsDetectionJobProperties": { "EndTime": number, "InputDataConfig": { "InputFormat": "string", "S3Uri": "string" }, "JobId": "string", "JobName": "string", "JobStatus": "string", "Message": "string", "NumberOfTopics": number, "OutputDataConfig": { "S3Uri": "string" }, "SubmitTime": number } }

Response Elements

If the action is successful, the service sends back an HTTP 200 response\.

The following data is returned in JSON format by the service\.

** [TopicsDetectionJobProperties](#API_DescribeTopicsDetectionJob_ResponseSyntax) **
The list of properties for the requested job\.
Type: [TopicsDetectionJobProperties](API_TopicsDetectionJobProperties.md) object

Errors

For information about the errors that are common to all actions, see [Common Errors](CommonErrors.md)\.

InternalServerException
An internal server error occurred\. Retry your request\.
HTTP Status Code: 500

InvalidRequestException
The request is invalid\.
HTTP Status Code: 400

JobNotFoundException
The specified job was not found\. Check the job ID and try again\.
HTTP Status Code: 400

TooManyRequestsException
The number of requests exceeds the limit\. Resubmit your request later\.
HTTP Status Code: 400

See Also

33

34 For more information about using this API in one of the language\-specific AWS SDKs, see the
following:

35

36 + [AWS Command Line Interface](http://docs.aws.amazon.com/goto/aws-cli/comprehend-2017-11-27/
DescribeTopicsDetectionJob)

37

38 + [AWS SDK for \.NET](http://docs.aws.amazon.com/goto/DotNetSDKV3/comprehend-2017-11-27/
DescribeTopicsDetectionJob)

39

40 + [AWS SDK for C\+\+](http://docs.aws.amazon.com/goto/SdkForCpp/comprehend-2017-11-27/
DescribeTopicsDetectionJob)

41

42 + [AWS SDK for Go](http://docs.aws.amazon.com/goto/SdkForGoV1/comprehend-2017-11-27/
DescribeTopicsDetectionJob)

43

44 + [AWS SDK for Java](http://docs.aws.amazon.com/goto/SdkForJava/comprehend-2017-11-27/
DescribeTopicsDetectionJob)

45

46 + [AWS SDK for JavaScript](http://docs.aws.amazon.com/goto/AWSJavaScriptSDK/comprehend
-2017-11-27/DescribeTopicsDetectionJob)

47

48 + [AWS SDK for PHP V3](http://docs.aws.amazon.com/goto/SdkForPHPV3/comprehend-2017-11-27/
DescribeTopicsDetectionJob)

49

50 + [AWS SDK for Python](http://docs.aws.amazon.com/goto/boto3/comprehend-2017-11-27/
DescribeTopicsDetectionJob)

51

52 + [AWS SDK for Ruby V2](http://docs.aws.amazon.com/goto/SdkForRubyV2/comprehend-2017-11-27/
DescribeTopicsDetectionJob)

53
54
55
56
57 # DetectDominantLanguage

58

59 Determines the dominant language of the input text\. For a list of languages that Amazon
Comprehend can detect, see [Amazon Comprehend Supported Languages](http://docs.aws.amazon.
com/comprehend/latest/dg/how-languages.html)\.

60

61 ## Request Syntax

{ "Text": "string" }

1

2 ## Request Parameters

3

4 For information about the parameters that are common to all actions, see [Common Parameters](
CommonParameters.md)\.

5

6 The request accepts the following data in JSON format\.

7

8 ** [Text](#API_DetectDominantLanguage_RequestSyntax) **   <a name="comprehend-
DetectDominantLanguage-request-Text"></a>

9 A UTF\-8 text string\. Each string should contain at least 20 characters and must contain fewer

```
    that 5,000 bytes of UTF\-8 encoded characters\.
10 Type: String
11 Length Constraints: Minimum length of 1\.
12 Required: Yes
13
14 ## Response Syntax<a name="API_DetectDominantLanguage_ResponseSyntax"></a>

   { "Languages": [ { "LanguageCode": "string", "Score": number } ] }

1
2 ## Response Elements<a name="API_DetectDominantLanguage_ResponseElements"></a>
3
4 If the action is successful, the service sends back an HTTP 200 response\.
5
6 The following data is returned in JSON format by the service\.
7
8  ** [Languages](#API_DetectDominantLanguage_ResponseSyntax) **   <a name="comprehend-
       DetectDominantLanguage-response-Languages"></a>
9 The languages that Amazon Comprehend detected in the input text\. For each language, the
       response returns the RFC 5646 language code and the level of confidence that Amazon
       Comprehend has in the accuracy of its inference\. For more information about RFC 5646, see [
       Tags for Identifying Languages](https://tools.ietf.org/html/rfc5646) on the *IETF Tools* web
       site\.
10 Type: Array of [DominantLanguage](API_DominantLanguage.md) objects
11
12 ## Errors<a name="API_DetectDominantLanguage_Errors"></a>
13
14 For information about the errors that are common to all actions, see [Common Errors](
       CommonErrors.md)\.
15
16  **InternalServerException**
17 An internal server error occurred\. Retry your request\.
18 HTTP Status Code: 500
19
20  **InvalidRequestException**
21 The request is invalid\.
22 HTTP Status Code: 400
23
24  **TextSizeLimitExceededException**
25 The size of the input text exceeds the limit\. Use a smaller document\.
26 HTTP Status Code: 400
27
28 ## Example<a name="API_DetectDominantLanguage_Examples"></a>
29
30 ### Detect dominant language<a name="API_DetectDominantLanguage_Example_1"></a>
31
32 If the input text is "Bob lives in Seattle\. He is a software engineer at Amazon\.", the
       operation returns the following:
33
34 #### <a name="w3ab1c22b5c23c15b3b5"></a>

   { "Languages": [ { "LanguageCode": "en", "Score": 0.9774383902549744 }, { "LanguageCode": "de", "Score":
     0.010717987082898617 } ] }

1
2 ## See Also<a name="API_DetectDominantLanguage_SeeAlso"></a>
```

For more information about using this API in one of the language\-specific AWS SDKs, see the following:

+   [AWS Command Line Interface](http://docs.aws.amazon.com/goto/aws-cli/comprehend-2017-11-27/DetectDominantLanguage)

+   [AWS SDK for \.NET](http://docs.aws.amazon.com/goto/DotNetSDKV3/comprehend-2017-11-27/DetectDominantLanguage)

+   [AWS SDK for C\+\+](http://docs.aws.amazon.com/goto/SdkForCpp/comprehend-2017-11-27/DetectDominantLanguage)

+   [AWS SDK for Go](http://docs.aws.amazon.com/goto/SdkForGoV1/comprehend-2017-11-27/DetectDominantLanguage)

+   [AWS SDK for Java](http://docs.aws.amazon.com/goto/SdkForJava/comprehend-2017-11-27/DetectDominantLanguage)

+   [AWS SDK for JavaScript](http://docs.aws.amazon.com/goto/AWSJavaScriptSDK/comprehend-2017-11-27/DetectDominantLanguage)

+   [AWS SDK for PHP V3](http://docs.aws.amazon.com/goto/SdkForPHPV3/comprehend-2017-11-27/DetectDominantLanguage)

+   [AWS SDK for Python](http://docs.aws.amazon.com/goto/boto3/comprehend-2017-11-27/DetectDominantLanguage)

+   [AWS SDK for Ruby V2](http://docs.aws.amazon.com/goto/SdkForRubyV2/comprehend-2017-11-27/DetectDominantLanguage)

DetectEntities

Inspects text for named entities, and returns information about them\. For more information, about named entities, see [Detecting Entities](how-entities.md)\.

Request Syntax

{ "LanguageCode": "string", "Text": "string" }

Request Parameters

For information about the parameters that are common to all actions, see [Common Parameters](CommonParameters.md)\.

The request accepts the following data in JSON format\.

 ** [LanguageCode](#API_DetectEntities_RequestSyntax) **
The language of the input documents\. You can specify English \("en"\) or Spanish \("es"\)\. All documents must be in the same language\.

10 Type: String
11 Valid Values:` en | es`
12 Required: Yes
13
14 ** [Text](#API_DetectEntities_RequestSyntax) **
15 A UTF\-8 text string\. Each string must contain fewer that 5,000 bytes of UTF\-8 encoded characters\.
16 Type: String
17 Length Constraints: Minimum length of 1\.
18 Required: Yes
19
20 ## Response Syntax

   { "Entities": [{ "BeginOffset": number, "EndOffset": number, "Score": number, "Text": "string", "Type": "string" }] }

1
2 ## Response Elements
3
4 If the action is successful, the service sends back an HTTP 200 response\.
5
6 The following data is returned in JSON format by the service\.
7
8 ** [Entities](#API_DetectEntities_ResponseSyntax) **
9 A collection of entities identified in the input text\. For each entity, the response provides the entity text, entity type, where the entity text begins and ends, and the level of confidence that Amazon Comprehend has in the detection\. For a list of entity types, see [Detecting Entities](how-entities.md)\.
10 Type: Array of [Entity](API_Entity.md) objects
11
12 ## Errors
13
14 For information about the errors that are common to all actions, see [Common Errors](CommonErrors.md)\.
15
16 **InternalServerException**
17 An internal server error occurred\. Retry your request\.
18 HTTP Status Code: 500
19
20 **InvalidRequestException**
21 The request is invalid\.
22 HTTP Status Code: 400
23
24 **TextSizeLimitExceededException**
25 The size of the input text exceeds the limit\. Use a smaller document\.
26 HTTP Status Code: 400
27
28 **UnsupportedLanguageException**
29 Amazon Comprehend can't process the language of the input text\. For all APIs except ` DetectDominantLanguage`, Amazon Comprehend accepts only English or Spanish text\. For the ` DetectDominantLanguage` API, Amazon Comprehend detects 100 languages\. For a list of languages, see [Detecting the Primary Language](how-languages.md)
30 HTTP Status Code: 400

31
32 ## Example

33
34 ### Detect entities

35
36 If the input text is "Bob ordered two sandwiches and three ice cream cones today from a store in
       Seattle\.", the operation returns the following:

37
38 ####

```
1  {
2  "Entities": [
3      {
4          "Text": "Bob",
5          "Score": 1.0,
6          "Type": "PERSON",
7          "BeginOffset": 0,
8          "EndOffset": 3
9      },
10     {
11         "Text": "two",
12         "Score": 1.0,
13         "Type": "QUANTITY",
14         "BeginOffset": 12,
15         "EndOffset": 15
16     },
17     {
18         "Text": "three",
19         "Score": 1.0,
20         "Type": "QUANTITY",
21         "BeginOffset": 32,
22         "EndOffset": 37
23     },
24     {
25         "Text": "Today",
26         "Score": 1.0,
27         "Type": "DATE",
28         "BeginOffset": 54,
29         "EndOffset": 59
30     },
31     {
32         "Text": "Seattle",
33         "Score": 1.0,
34         "Type": "LOCATION",
35         "BeginOffset": 76,
36         "EndOffset": 83
37     }
38 ],

   }

```

1
2 ## See Also

3
4 For more information about using this API in one of the language\-specific AWS SDKs, see the
       following:

6 + [AWS Command Line Interface](http://docs.aws.amazon.com/goto/aws-cli/comprehend-2017-11-27/
    DetectEntities)

7

8 + [AWS SDK for \.NET](http://docs.aws.amazon.com/goto/DotNetSDKV3/comprehend-2017-11-27/
    DetectEntities)

9

10 + [AWS SDK for C\+\+](http://docs.aws.amazon.com/goto/SdkForCpp/comprehend-2017-11-27/
    DetectEntities)

11

12 + [AWS SDK for Go](http://docs.aws.amazon.com/goto/SdkForGoV1/comprehend-2017-11-27/
    DetectEntities)

13

14 + [AWS SDK for Java](http://docs.aws.amazon.com/goto/SdkForJava/comprehend-2017-11-27/
    DetectEntities)

15

16 + [AWS SDK for JavaScript](http://docs.aws.amazon.com/goto/AWSJavaScriptSDK/comprehend
    -2017-11-27/DetectEntities)

17

18 + [AWS SDK for PHP V3](http://docs.aws.amazon.com/goto/SdkForPHPV3/comprehend-2017-11-27/
    DetectEntities)

19

20 + [AWS SDK for Python](http://docs.aws.amazon.com/goto/boto3/comprehend-2017-11-27/
    DetectEntities)

21

22 + [AWS SDK for Ruby V2](http://docs.aws.amazon.com/goto/SdkForRubyV2/comprehend-2017-11-27/
    DetectEntities)

23

24

25

26

27 # DetectKeyPhrases

28

29 Detects the key noun phrases found in the text\.

30

31 ## Request Syntax

   { "LanguageCode": "string", "Text": "string" }

1

2 ## Request Parameters

3

4 For information about the parameters that are common to all actions, see [Common Parameters](
    CommonParameters.md)\.

5

6 The request accepts the following data in JSON format\.

7

8 ** [LanguageCode](#API_DetectKeyPhrases_RequestSyntax) **   <a name="comprehend-
    DetectKeyPhrases-request-LanguageCode"></a>

9 The language of the input documents\. You can specify English \("en"\) or Spanish \("es"\)\. All
    documents must be in the same language\.

10 Type: String

11 Valid Values:` en | es`

12 Required: Yes

13

14 ** [Text](#API_DetectKeyPhrases_RequestSyntax) **

15 A UTF\-8 text string\. Each string must contain fewer that 5,000 bytes of UTF\-8 encoded characters\.

16 Type: String

17 Length Constraints: Minimum length of 1\.

18 Required: Yes

19

20 ## Response Syntax

{ "KeyPhrases": [{ "BeginOffset": number, "EndOffset": number, "Score": number, "Text": "string" }] }

1

2 ## Response Elements

3

4 If the action is successful, the service sends back an HTTP 200 response\.

5

6 The following data is returned in JSON format by the service\.

7

8 ** [KeyPhrases](#API_DetectKeyPhrases_ResponseSyntax) **

9 A collection of key phrases that Amazon Comprehend identified in the input text\. For each key phrase, the response provides the text of the key phrase, where the key phrase begins and ends, and the level of confidence that Amazon Comprehend has in the accuracy of the detection\.

10 Type: Array of [KeyPhrase](API_KeyPhrase.md) objects

11

12 ## Errors

13

14 For information about the errors that are common to all actions, see [Common Errors](CommonErrors.md)\.

15

16 **InternalServerException**

17 An internal server error occurred\. Retry your request\.

18 HTTP Status Code: 500

19

20 **InvalidRequestException**

21 The request is invalid\.

22 HTTP Status Code: 400

23

24 **TextSizeLimitExceededException**

25 The size of the input text exceeds the limit\. Use a smaller document\.

26 HTTP Status Code: 400

27

28 **UnsupportedLanguageException**

29 Amazon Comprehend can't process the language of the input text\. For all APIs except `DetectDominantLanguage`, Amazon Comprehend accepts only English or Spanish text\. For the `DetectDominantLanguage` API, Amazon Comprehend detects 100 languages\. For a list of languages, see [Detecting the Primary Language](how-languages.md)

30 HTTP Status Code: 400

31

32 ## Example

33

34 ### Detect phrases

35

36 If the input text is "Bob lives in Seattle\. He is a software engineer at Amazon\.", the API
returns the following:

37

38 ####

```
1        {
2  "KeyPhrases": [
3      {
4          "Text": "Bob",
5          "Score": 1.0,
6          "BeginOffset": 0,
7          "EndOffset": 3
8      },
9      {
10          "Text": "Seattle",
11          "Score": 1.0,
12          "BeginOffset": 13,
13          "EndOffset": 20
14      },
15      {
16          "Text": "an engineer",
17          "Score": 1.0,
18          "BeginOffset": 28,
19          "EndOffset": 39
20      },
21      {
22          "Text": "Amazon",
23          "Score": 1.0,
24          "BeginOffset": 43,
25          "EndOffset": 49
26      }
27  ]

   }}
```

1

2 ## See Also

3

4 For more information about using this API in one of the language\-specific AWS SDKs, see the
following:

5

6 +   [AWS Command Line Interface](http://docs.aws.amazon.com/goto/aws-cli/comprehend-2017-11-27/
DetectKeyPhrases)

7

8 +   [AWS SDK for \.NET](http://docs.aws.amazon.com/goto/DotNetSDKV3/comprehend-2017-11-27/
DetectKeyPhrases)

9

10 +   [AWS SDK for C\+\+](http://docs.aws.amazon.com/goto/SdkForCpp/comprehend-2017-11-27/
DetectKeyPhrases)

11

12 +   [AWS SDK for Go](http://docs.aws.amazon.com/goto/SdkForGoV1/comprehend-2017-11-27/
DetectKeyPhrases)

13

14 +   [AWS SDK for Java](http://docs.aws.amazon.com/goto/SdkForJava/comprehend-2017-11-27/
DetectKeyPhrases)

```
15
16 +   [AWS SDK for JavaScript](http://docs.aws.amazon.com/goto/AWSJavaScriptSDK/comprehend
        -2017-11-27/DetectKeyPhrases)
17
18 +   [AWS SDK for PHP V3](http://docs.aws.amazon.com/goto/SdkForPHPV3/comprehend-2017-11-27/
        DetectKeyPhrases)
19
20 +   [AWS SDK for Python](http://docs.aws.amazon.com/goto/boto3/comprehend-2017-11-27/
        DetectKeyPhrases)
21
22 +   [AWS SDK for Ruby V2](http://docs.aws.amazon.com/goto/SdkForRubyV2/comprehend-2017-11-27/
        DetectKeyPhrases)
23
24
25
26
27 # DetectSentiment<a name="API_DetectSentiment"></a>
28
29 Inspects text and returns an inference of the prevailing sentiment \(`POSITIVE`, `NEUTRAL`, `
        MIXED`, or `NEGATIVE`\)\.
30
31 ## Request Syntax<a name="API_DetectSentiment_RequestSyntax"></a>

   { "LanguageCode": "string", "Text": "string" }

1
2 ## Request Parameters<a name="API_DetectSentiment_RequestParameters"></a>
3
4 For information about the parameters that are common to all actions, see [Common Parameters](
        CommonParameters.md)\.
5
6 The request accepts the following data in JSON format\.
7
8  ** [LanguageCode](#API_DetectSentiment_RequestSyntax) **   <a name="comprehend-DetectSentiment-
        request-LanguageCode"></a>
9 The language of the input documents\. You can specify English \("en"\) or Spanish \("es"\)\. All
        documents must be in the same language\.
10 Type: String
11 Valid Values:` en | es`
12 Required: Yes
13
14  ** [Text](#API_DetectSentiment_RequestSyntax) **   <a name="comprehend-DetectSentiment-request-
        Text"></a>
15 A UTF\-8 text string\. Each string must contain fewer that 5,000 bytes of UTF\-8 encoded
        characters\.
16 Type: String
17 Length Constraints: Minimum length of 1\.
18 Required: Yes
19
20 ## Response Syntax<a name="API_DetectSentiment_ResponseSyntax"></a>

   { "Sentiment": "string", "SentimentScore": { "Mixed": number, "Negative": number, "Neutral": number,
   "Positive": number } }

1
2 ## Response Elements<a name="API_DetectSentiment_ResponseElements"></a>
```

3
4 If the action is successful, the service sends back an HTTP 200 response\.

5
6 The following data is returned in JSON format by the service\.

7
8 ** [Sentiment](#API_DetectSentiment_ResponseSyntax) **
9 The inferred sentiment that Amazon Comprehend has the highest level of confidence in\.
10 Type: String
11 Valid Values:` POSITIVE | NEGATIVE | NEUTRAL | MIXED`

12
13 ** [SentimentScore](#API_DetectSentiment_ResponseSyntax) **
14 An object that lists the sentiments, and their corresponding confidence levels\.
15 Type: [SentimentScore](API_SentimentScore.md) object

16
17 ## Errors

18
19 For information about the errors that are common to all actions, see [Common Errors](CommonErrors.md)\.

20
21 **InternalServerException**
22 An internal server error occurred\. Retry your request\.
23 HTTP Status Code: 500

24
25 **InvalidRequestException**
26 The request is invalid\.
27 HTTP Status Code: 400

28
29 **TextSizeLimitExceededException**
30 The size of the input text exceeds the limit\. Use a smaller document\.
31 HTTP Status Code: 400

32
33 **UnsupportedLanguageException**
34 Amazon Comprehend can't process the language of the input text\. For all APIs except `DetectDominantLanguage`, Amazon Comprehend accepts only English or Spanish text\. For the `DetectDominantLanguage` API, Amazon Comprehend detects 100 languages\. For a list of languages, see [Detecting the Primary Language](how-languages.md)
35 HTTP Status Code: 400

36
37 ## Example

38
39 ### Detect sentiment

40
41 If the input text is "Today is my birthday, I am so happy\.", the operation returns the following response:

42
43 ####

{ "SentimentScore": { "Mixed": 0.0033542951568961143, "Positive": 0.9869875907897949, "Neutral": 0.008563132025301456, "Negative": 0.0010949420975521207 }, "Sentiment": "POSITIVE", }
}

1
2 ## See Also

For more information about using this API in one of the language\-specific AWS SDKs, see the following:

+ [AWS Command Line Interface](http://docs.aws.amazon.com/goto/aws-cli/comprehend-2017-11-27/DetectSentiment)

+ [AWS SDK for \.NET](http://docs.aws.amazon.com/goto/DotNetSDKV3/comprehend-2017-11-27/DetectSentiment)

+ [AWS SDK for C\+\+](http://docs.aws.amazon.com/goto/SdkForCpp/comprehend-2017-11-27/DetectSentiment)

+ [AWS SDK for Go](http://docs.aws.amazon.com/goto/SdkForGoV1/comprehend-2017-11-27/DetectSentiment)

+ [AWS SDK for Java](http://docs.aws.amazon.com/goto/SdkForJava/comprehend-2017-11-27/DetectSentiment)

+ [AWS SDK for JavaScript](http://docs.aws.amazon.com/goto/AWSJavaScriptSDK/comprehend-2017-11-27/DetectSentiment)

+ [AWS SDK for PHP V3](http://docs.aws.amazon.com/goto/SdkForPHPV3/comprehend-2017-11-27/DetectSentiment)

+ [AWS SDK for Python](http://docs.aws.amazon.com/goto/boto3/comprehend-2017-11-27/DetectSentiment)

+ [AWS SDK for Ruby V2](http://docs.aws.amazon.com/goto/SdkForRubyV2/comprehend-2017-11-27/DetectSentiment)

ListTopicsDetectionJobs

Gets a list of the topic detection jobs that you have submitted\.

Request Syntax

{ "Filter": { "JobName": "string", "JobStatus": "string", "SubmitTimeAfter": number, "SubmitTimeBefore": number }, "MaxResults": number, "NextToken": "string" }

Request Parameters

For information about the parameters that are common to all actions, see [Common Parameters](CommonParameters.md)\.

The request accepts the following data in JSON format\.

** [Filter](#API_ListTopicsDetectionJobs_RequestSyntax) **
Filters the jobs that are returned\. Jobs can be filtered on their name, status, or the date and time that they were submitted\. You can set only one filter at a time\.

10 Type: [TopicsDetectionJobFilter](API_TopicsDetectionJobFilter.md) object
11 Required: No
12
13 ** [MaxResults](#API_ListTopicsDetectionJobs_RequestSyntax) **   <a name="comprehend-
    ListTopicsDetectionJobs-request-MaxResults"></a>
14 The maximum number of results to return in each page\.
15 Type: Integer
16 Valid Range: Minimum value of 1\. Maximum value of 500\.
17 Required: No
18
19 ** [NextToken](#API_ListTopicsDetectionJobs_RequestSyntax) **   <a name="comprehend-
    ListTopicsDetectionJobs-request-NextToken"></a>
20 Identifies the next page of results to return\.
21 Type: String
22 Length Constraints: Minimum length of 1\.
23 Required: No
24
25 ## Response Syntax

{ "NextToken": "string", "TopicsDetectionJobPropertiesList": [{ "EndTime": number, "InputDataConfig": { "InputFormat": "string", "S3Uri": "string" }, "JobId": "string", "JobName": "string", "JobStatus": "string", "Message": "string", "NumberOfTopics": number, "OutputDataConfig": { "S3Uri": "string" }, "SubmitTime": number }] }

1
2 ## Response Elements
3
4 If the action is successful, the service sends back an HTTP 200 response\.
5
6 The following data is returned in JSON format by the service\.
7
8 ** [NextToken](#API_ListTopicsDetectionJobs_ResponseSyntax) **   <a name="comprehend-
    ListTopicsDetectionJobs-response-NextToken"></a>
9 Identifies the next page of results to return\.
10 Type: String
11 Length Constraints: Minimum length of 1\.
12
13 ** [TopicsDetectionJobPropertiesList](#API_ListTopicsDetectionJobs_ResponseSyntax) **   <a name
    ="comprehend-ListTopicsDetectionJobs-response-TopicsDetectionJobPropertiesList"></a>
14 A list containing the properties of each job that is returned\.
15 Type: Array of [TopicsDetectionJobProperties](API_TopicsDetectionJobProperties.md) objects
16
17 ## Errors
18
19 For information about the errors that are common to all actions, see [Common Errors](
    CommonErrors.md)\.
20
21 **InternalServerException**
22 An internal server error occurred\. Retry your request\.
23 HTTP Status Code: 500
24
25 **InvalidFilterException**
26 The filter specified for the `ListTopicDetectionJobs` operation is invalid\. Specify a different
    filter\.
27 HTTP Status Code: 400

28

29 **InvalidRequestException**

30 The request is invalid\.

31 HTTP Status Code: 400

32

33 **TooManyRequestsException**

34 The number of requests exceeds the limit\. Resubmit your request later\.

35 HTTP Status Code: 400

36

37 ## See Also

38

39 For more information about using this API in one of the language\-specific AWS SDKs, see the
   following:

40

41 + [AWS Command Line Interface](http://docs.aws.amazon.com/goto/aws-cli/comprehend-2017-11-27/
   ListTopicsDetectionJobs)

42

43 + [AWS SDK for \.NET](http://docs.aws.amazon.com/goto/DotNetSDKV3/comprehend-2017-11-27/
   ListTopicsDetectionJobs)

44

45 + [AWS SDK for C\+\+](http://docs.aws.amazon.com/goto/SdkForCpp/comprehend-2017-11-27/
   ListTopicsDetectionJobs)

46

47 + [AWS SDK for Go](http://docs.aws.amazon.com/goto/SdkForGoV1/comprehend-2017-11-27/
   ListTopicsDetectionJobs)

48

49 + [AWS SDK for Java](http://docs.aws.amazon.com/goto/SdkForJava/comprehend-2017-11-27/
   ListTopicsDetectionJobs)

50

51 + [AWS SDK for JavaScript](http://docs.aws.amazon.com/goto/AWSJavaScriptSDK/comprehend
   -2017-11-27/ListTopicsDetectionJobs)

52

53 + [AWS SDK for PHP V3](http://docs.aws.amazon.com/goto/SdkForPHPV3/comprehend-2017-11-27/
   ListTopicsDetectionJobs)

54

55 + [AWS SDK for Python](http://docs.aws.amazon.com/goto/boto3/comprehend-2017-11-27/
   ListTopicsDetectionJobs)

56

57 + [AWS SDK for Ruby V2](http://docs.aws.amazon.com/goto/SdkForRubyV2/comprehend-2017-11-27/
   ListTopicsDetectionJobs)

58

59

60

61

62 # StartTopicsDetectionJob

63

64 Starts an asynchronous topic detection job\. Use the `DescribeTopicDetectionJob` operation to
   track the status of a job\.

65

66 ## Request Syntax

{ "ClientRequestToken": "string", "DataAccessRoleArn": "string", "InputDataConfig": { "InputFormat":
"string", "S3Uri": "string" }, "JobName": "string", "NumberOfTopics": number, "OutputDataConfig": {
"S3Uri": "string" } }

Request Parameters

For information about the parameters that are common to all actions, see [Common Parameters](CommonParameters.md)\.

The request accepts the following data in JSON format\.

** [ClientRequestToken](#API_StartTopicsDetectionJob_RequestSyntax) **
A unique identifier for the request\. If you do not set the client request token, Amazon Comprehend generates one\.
Type: String
Length Constraints: Minimum length of 1\. Maximum length of 64\.
Pattern: `^[a-zA-Z0-9-]+$`
Required: No

** [DataAccessRoleArn](#API_StartTopicsDetectionJob_RequestSyntax) **
The Amazon Resource Name \(ARN\) of the AWS Identity and Access Management \(IAM\) role that grants Amazon Comprehend read access to your input data\.
Type: String
Pattern: `arn:aws(-[^:]+)?:iam::[0-9]{12}:role/.+`
Required: Yes

** [InputDataConfig](#API_StartTopicsDetectionJob_RequestSyntax) **
Specifies the format and location of the input data for the job\.
Type: [InputDataConfig](API_InputDataConfig.md) object
Required: Yes

** [JobName](#API_StartTopicsDetectionJob_RequestSyntax) **
The identifier of the job\.
Type: String
Length Constraints: Minimum length of 1\. Maximum length of 256\.
Pattern: `^([\p{L}\p{Z}\p{N}_.:/=+\-%@]*)$`
Required: No

** [NumberOfTopics](#API_StartTopicsDetectionJob_RequestSyntax) **
The number of topics to detect\.
Type: Integer
Valid Range: Minimum value of 1\. Maximum value of 100\.
Required: No

** [OutputDataConfig](#API_StartTopicsDetectionJob_RequestSyntax) **
Specifies where to send the output files\.
Type: [OutputDataConfig](API_OutputDataConfig.md) object
Required: Yes

Response Syntax

{ "JobId": "string", "JobStatus": "string" }

Response Elements

If the action is successful, the service sends back an HTTP 200 response\.

The following data is returned in JSON format by the service\.

 ** [JobId](#API_StartTopicsDetectionJob_ResponseSyntax) **
The identifier generated for the job\. To get the status of the job, use this identifier with the `DescribeTopicDetectionJob` operation\.
Type: String
Length Constraints: Minimum length of 1\. Maximum length of 32\.

 ** [JobStatus](#API_StartTopicsDetectionJob_ResponseSyntax) **
The status of the job:

+ SUBMITTED \- The job has been received and is queued for processing\.

+ IN_PROGRESS \- Amazon Comprehend is processing the job\.

+ COMPLETED \- The job was successfully completed and the output is available\.

+ FAILED \- The job did not complete\. To get details, use the `DescribeTopicDetectionJob` operation\.
Type: String
Valid Values:` SUBMITTED | IN_PROGRESS | COMPLETED | FAILED`

Errors

For information about the errors that are common to all actions, see [Common Errors](CommonErrors.md)\.

 InternalServerException
An internal server error occurred\. Retry your request\.
HTTP Status Code: 500

 InvalidRequestException
The request is invalid\.
HTTP Status Code: 400

 TooManyRequestsException
The number of requests exceeds the limit\. Resubmit your request later\.
HTTP Status Code: 400

See Also

For more information about using this API in one of the language\-specific AWS SDKs, see the following:

+   [AWS Command Line Interface](http://docs.aws.amazon.com/goto/aws-cli/comprehend-2017-11-27/StartTopicsDetectionJob)

48 + [AWS SDK for \.NET](http://docs.aws.amazon.com/goto/DotNetSDKV3/comprehend-2017-11-27/
   StartTopicsDetectionJob)

49
50 + [AWS SDK for C\+\+](http://docs.aws.amazon.com/goto/SdkForCpp/comprehend-2017-11-27/
   StartTopicsDetectionJob)

51
52 + [AWS SDK for Go](http://docs.aws.amazon.com/goto/SdkForGoV1/comprehend-2017-11-27/
   StartTopicsDetectionJob)

53
54 + [AWS SDK for Java](http://docs.aws.amazon.com/goto/SdkForJava/comprehend-2017-11-27/
   StartTopicsDetectionJob)

55
56 + [AWS SDK for JavaScript](http://docs.aws.amazon.com/goto/AWSJavaScriptSDK/comprehend
   -2017-11-27/StartTopicsDetectionJob)

57
58 + [AWS SDK for PHP V3](http://docs.aws.amazon.com/goto/SdkForPHPV3/comprehend-2017-11-27/
   StartTopicsDetectionJob)

59
60 + [AWS SDK for Python](http://docs.aws.amazon.com/goto/boto3/comprehend-2017-11-27/
   StartTopicsDetectionJob)

61
62 + [AWS SDK for Ruby V2](http://docs.aws.amazon.com/goto/SdkForRubyV2/comprehend-2017-11-27/
   StartTopicsDetectionJob)

63
64
65
66
67 # Data Types
68
69 The following data types are supported:
70
71 + [BatchDetectDominantLanguageItemResult](API_BatchDetectDominantLanguageItemResult.md)
72
73 + [BatchDetectEntitiesItemResult](API_BatchDetectEntitiesItemResult.md)
74
75 + [BatchDetectKeyPhrasesItemResult](API_BatchDetectKeyPhrasesItemResult.md)
76
77 + [BatchDetectSentimentItemResult](API_BatchDetectSentimentItemResult.md)
78
79 + [BatchItemError](API_BatchItemError.md)
80
81 + [DominantLanguage](API_DominantLanguage.md)
82
83 + [Entity](API_Entity.md)
84
85 + [InputDataConfig](API_InputDataConfig.md)
86
87 + [KeyPhrase](API_KeyPhrase.md)
88
89 + [OutputDataConfig](API_OutputDataConfig.md)
90
91 + [SentimentScore](API_SentimentScore.md)
92
93 + [TopicsDetectionJobFilter](API_TopicsDetectionJobFilter.md)

```
94
95 +   [TopicsDetectionJobProperties](API_TopicsDetectionJobProperties.md)
96
97
98
99
100 # BatchDetectDominantLanguageItemResult<a name="API_BatchDetectDominantLanguageItemResult"></a>
101
102 The result of calling the [BatchDetectDominantLanguage](API_BatchDetectDominantLanguage.md)
        operation\. The operation returns one object for each document that is successfully
        processed by the operation\.
103
104 ## Contents<a name="API_BatchDetectDominantLanguageItemResult_Contents"></a>
105
106  **Index**    <a name="comprehend-Type-BatchDetectDominantLanguageItemResult-Index"></a>
107 The zero\-based index of the document in the input list\.
108 Type: Integer
109 Required: No
110
111  **Languages**    <a name="comprehend-Type-BatchDetectDominantLanguageItemResult-Languages"></a>
112 One or more [DominantLanguage](API_DominantLanguage.md) objects describing the dominant
        languages in the document\.
113 Type: Array of [DominantLanguage](API_DominantLanguage.md) objects
114 Required: No
115
116 ## See Also<a name="API_BatchDetectDominantLanguageItemResult_SeeAlso"></a>
117
118 For more information about using this API in one of the language\-specific AWS SDKs, see the
        following:
119
120 +   [AWS SDK for C\+\+](http://docs.aws.amazon.com/goto/SdkForCpp/comprehend-2017-11-27/
        BatchDetectDominantLanguageItemResult)
121
122 +   [AWS SDK for Go](http://docs.aws.amazon.com/goto/SdkForGoV1/comprehend-2017-11-27/
        BatchDetectDominantLanguageItemResult)
123
124 +   [AWS SDK for Java](http://docs.aws.amazon.com/goto/SdkForJava/comprehend-2017-11-27/
        BatchDetectDominantLanguageItemResult)
125
126 +   [AWS SDK for Ruby V2](http://docs.aws.amazon.com/goto/SdkForRubyV2/comprehend-2017-11-27/
        BatchDetectDominantLanguageItemResult)
127
128
129
130
131 # BatchDetectEntitiesItemResult<a name="API_BatchDetectEntitiesItemResult"></a>
132
133 The result of calling the [BatchDetectKeyPhrases](API_BatchDetectKeyPhrases.md) operation\. The
        operation returns one object for each document that is successfully processed by the
        operation\.
134
135 ## Contents<a name="API_BatchDetectEntitiesItemResult_Contents"></a>
136
137  **Entities**    <a name="comprehend-Type-BatchDetectEntitiesItemResult-Entities"></a>
```

One or more [Entity](API_Entity.md) objects, one for each entity detected in the document\.
Type: Array of [Entity](API_Entity.md) objects
Required: No

Index
The zero\-based index of the document in the input list\.
Type: Integer
Required: No

See Also

For more information about using this API in one of the language\-specific AWS SDKs, see the
    following:

+   [AWS SDK for C\+\+](http://docs.aws.amazon.com/goto/SdkForCpp/comprehend-2017-11-27/
    BatchDetectEntitiesItemResult)

+   [AWS SDK for Go](http://docs.aws.amazon.com/goto/SdkForGoV1/comprehend-2017-11-27/
    BatchDetectEntitiesItemResult)

+   [AWS SDK for Java](http://docs.aws.amazon.com/goto/SdkForJava/comprehend-2017-11-27/
    BatchDetectEntitiesItemResult)

+   [AWS SDK for Ruby V2](http://docs.aws.amazon.com/goto/SdkForRubyV2/comprehend-2017-11-27/
    BatchDetectEntitiesItemResult)

BatchDetectKeyPhrasesItemResult

The result of calling the [BatchDetectKeyPhrases](API_BatchDetectKeyPhrases.md) operation\. The
    operation returns one object for each document that is successfully processed by the
    operation\.

Contents

Index
The zero\-based index of the document in the input list\.
Type: Integer
Required: No

KeyPhrases
One or more [KeyPhrase](API_KeyPhrase.md) objects, one for each key phrase detected in the
    document\.
Type: Array of [KeyPhrase](API_KeyPhrase.md) objects
Required: No

See Also

For more information about using this API in one of the language\-specific AWS SDKs, see the
    following:

+   [AWS SDK for C\+\+](http://docs.aws.amazon.com/goto/SdkForCpp/comprehend-2017-11-27/

```
BatchDetectKeyPhrasesItemResult)
```
183

184 + [AWS SDK for Go](http://docs.aws.amazon.com/goto/SdkForGoV1/comprehend-2017-11-27/
   BatchDetectKeyPhrasesItemResult)

185

186 + [AWS SDK for Java](http://docs.aws.amazon.com/goto/SdkForJava/comprehend-2017-11-27/
   BatchDetectKeyPhrasesItemResult)

187

188 + [AWS SDK for Ruby V2](http://docs.aws.amazon.com/goto/SdkForRubyV2/comprehend-2017-11-27/
   BatchDetectKeyPhrasesItemResult)

189

190

191

192

193 # BatchDetectSentimentItemResult

194

195 The result of calling the [BatchDetectSentiment](API_BatchDetectSentiment.md) operation\. The
   operation returns one object for each document that is successfully processed by the
   operation\.

196

197 ## Contents

198

199 **Index**

200 The zero\-based index of the document in the input list\.

201 Type: Integer

202 Required: No

203

204 **Sentiment**

205 The sentiment detected in the document\.

206 Type: String

207 Valid Values:` POSITIVE | NEGATIVE | NEUTRAL | MIXED`

208 Required: No

209

210 **SentimentScore**

211 The level of confidence that Amazon Comprehend has in the accuracy of its sentiment detection\.

212 Type: [SentimentScore](API_SentimentScore.md) object

213 Required: No

214

215 ## See Also

216

217 For more information about using this API in one of the language\-specific AWS SDKs, see the
   following:

218

219 + [AWS SDK for C\+\+](http://docs.aws.amazon.com/goto/SdkForCpp/comprehend-2017-11-27/
   BatchDetectSentimentItemResult)

220

221 + [AWS SDK for Go](http://docs.aws.amazon.com/goto/SdkForGoV1/comprehend-2017-11-27/
   BatchDetectSentimentItemResult)

222

223 + [AWS SDK for Java](http://docs.aws.amazon.com/goto/SdkForJava/comprehend-2017-11-27/
   BatchDetectSentimentItemResult)

224

225 + [AWS SDK for Ruby V2](http://docs.aws.amazon.com/goto/SdkForRubyV2/comprehend-2017-11-27/

```
        BatchDetectSentimentItemResult)
226
227
228
229
230 # BatchItemError<a name="API_BatchItemError"></a>
231
232 Describes an error that occurred while processing a document in a batch\. The operation returns
        on `BatchItemError` object for each document that contained an error\.
233
234 ## Contents<a name="API_BatchItemError_Contents"></a>
235
236  **ErrorCode**    <a name="comprehend-Type-BatchItemError-ErrorCode"></a>
237 The numeric error code of the error\.
238 Type: String
239 Length Constraints: Minimum length of 1\.
240 Required: No
241
242  **ErrorMessage**    <a name="comprehend-Type-BatchItemError-ErrorMessage"></a>
243 A text description of the error\.
244 Type: String
245 Length Constraints: Minimum length of 1\.
246 Required: No
247
248  **Index**    <a name="comprehend-Type-BatchItemError-Index"></a>
249 The zero\-based index of the document in the input list\.
250 Type: Integer
251 Required: No
252
253 ## See Also<a name="API_BatchItemError_SeeAlso"></a>
254
255 For more information about using this API in one of the language\-specific AWS SDKs, see the
        following:
256
257 +   [AWS SDK for C\+\+](http://docs.aws.amazon.com/goto/SdkForCpp/comprehend-2017-11-27/
        BatchItemError)
258
259 +   [AWS SDK for Go](http://docs.aws.amazon.com/goto/SdkForGoV1/comprehend-2017-11-27/
        BatchItemError)
260
261 +   [AWS SDK for Java](http://docs.aws.amazon.com/goto/SdkForJava/comprehend-2017-11-27/
        BatchItemError)
262
263 +   [AWS SDK for Ruby V2](http://docs.aws.amazon.com/goto/SdkForRubyV2/comprehend-2017-11-27/
        BatchItemError)
264
265
266
267
268 # DominantLanguage<a name="API_DominantLanguage"></a>
269
270 Returns the code for the dominant language in the input text and the level of confidence that
        Amazon Comprehend has in the accuracy of the detection\.
271
```

Contents

LanguageCode
The RFC 5646 language code for the dominant language\. For more information about RFC 5646, see [Tags for Identifying Languages](https://tools.ietf.org/html/rfc5646) on the *IETF Tools* web site\.
Type: String
Length Constraints: Minimum length of 1\.
Required: No

Score
The level of confidence that Amazon Comprehend has in the accuracy of the detection\.
Type: Float
Required: No

See Also

For more information about using this API in one of the language\-specific AWS SDKs, see the following:

+ [AWS SDK for C\+\+](http://docs.aws.amazon.com/goto/SdkForCpp/comprehend-2017-11-27/DominantLanguage)

+ [AWS SDK for Go](http://docs.aws.amazon.com/goto/SdkForGoV1/comprehend-2017-11-27/DominantLanguage)

+ [AWS SDK for Java](http://docs.aws.amazon.com/goto/SdkForJava/comprehend-2017-11-27/DominantLanguage)

+ [AWS SDK for Ruby V2](http://docs.aws.amazon.com/goto/SdkForRubyV2/comprehend-2017-11-27/DominantLanguage)

Entity

Provides information about an entity\.

Contents

BeginOffset
A character offset in the input text that shows where the entity begins \(the first character is at position 0\)\. The offset returns the position of each UTF\-8 code point in the string\. A *code point* is the abstract character from a particular graphical representation\. For example, a multi\-byte UTF\-8 character maps to a single code point\.
Type: Integer
Required: No

EndOffset
A character offset in the input text that shows where the entity ends\. The offset returns the position of each UTF\-8 code point in the string\. A *code point* is the abstract character

from a particular graphical representation\. For example, a multi\-byte UTF\-8 character
maps to a single code point\.

Type: Integer

Required: No

 Score

The level of confidence that Amazon Comprehend has in the accuracy of the detection\.

Type: Float

Required: No

 Text

The text of the entity\.

Type: String

Length Constraints: Minimum length of 1\.

Required: No

 Type

The entity's type\.

Type: String

Valid Values:` PERSON | LOCATION | ORGANIZATION | COMMERCIAL_ITEM | EVENT | DATE | QUANTITY |
TITLE | OTHER`

Required: No

See Also

For more information about using this API in one of the language\-specific AWS SDKs, see the
following:

+   [AWS SDK for C\+\+] (http://docs.aws.amazon.com/goto/SdkForCpp/comprehend-2017-11-27/Entity)

+   [AWS SDK for Go] (http://docs.aws.amazon.com/goto/SdkForGoV1/comprehend-2017-11-27/Entity)

+   [AWS SDK for Java] (http://docs.aws.amazon.com/goto/SdkForJava/comprehend-2017-11-27/Entity)

+   [AWS SDK for Ruby V2] (http://docs.aws.amazon.com/goto/SdkForRubyV2/comprehend-2017-11-27/
Entity)

InputDataConfig

The input properties for a topic detection job\.

Contents

 InputFormat

Specifies how the text in an input file should be processed:

+   `ONE_DOC_PER_FILE` \- Each file is considered a separate document\. Use this option when you
are processing large documents, such as newspaper articles or scientific papers\.

+   `ONE_DOC_PER_LINE` \- Each line in a file is considered a separate document\. Use this option
when you are processing many short documents, such as text messages\.

362 Type: String
363 Valid Values:` ONE_DOC_PER_FILE | ONE_DOC_PER_LINE`
364 Required: No
365
366 **S3Uri**
367 The Amazon S3 URI for the input data\. The URI must be in same region as the API endpoint that you are calling\. The URI can point to a single input file or it can provide the prefix for a collection of data files\.
368 For example, if you use the URI `S3://bucketName/prefix`, if the prefix is a single file, Amazon Comprehend uses that file as input\. If more than one file begins with the prefix, Amazon Comprehend uses all of them as input\.
369 Type: String
370 Length Constraints: Maximum length of 1024\.
371 Pattern: `s3://([^/]+)(/.*)?`
372 Required: Yes
373
374 ## See Also
375
376 For more information about using this API in one of the language\-specific AWS SDKs, see the following:
377
378 +   [AWS SDK for C\+\+](http://docs.aws.amazon.com/goto/SdkForCpp/comprehend-2017-11-27/InputDataConfig)
379
380 +   [AWS SDK for Go](http://docs.aws.amazon.com/goto/SdkForGoV1/comprehend-2017-11-27/InputDataConfig)
381
382 +   [AWS SDK for Java](http://docs.aws.amazon.com/goto/SdkForJava/comprehend-2017-11-27/InputDataConfig)
383
384 +   [AWS SDK for Ruby V2](http://docs.aws.amazon.com/goto/SdkForRubyV2/comprehend-2017-11-27/InputDataConfig)
385
386
387
388
389 # KeyPhrase
390
391 Describes a key noun phrase\.
392
393 ## Contents
394
395 **BeginOffset**
396 A character offset in the input text that shows where the key phrase begins \(the first character is at position 0\)\. The offset returns the position of each UTF\-8 code point in the string\. A *code point* is the abstract character from a particular graphical representation\. For example, a multi\-byte UTF\-8 character maps to a single code point\.
397 Type: Integer
398 Required: No
399
400 **EndOffset**
401 A character offset in the input text where the key phrase ends\. The offset returns the position of each UTF\-8 code point in the string\. A `code point` is the abstract character from a particular graphical representation\. For example, a multi\-byte UTF\-8 character maps to a

single code point\.

Type: Integer

Required: No

Score
The level of confidence that Amazon Comprehend has in the accuracy of the detection\.

Type: Float

Required: No

Text
The text of a key noun phrase\.

Type: String

Length Constraints: Minimum length of 1\.

Required: No

See Also

For more information about using this API in one of the language\-specific AWS SDKs, see the following:

+ [AWS SDK for C\+\+](http://docs.aws.amazon.com/goto/SdkForCpp/comprehend-2017-11-27/KeyPhrase)

+ [AWS SDK for Go](http://docs.aws.amazon.com/goto/SdkForGoV1/comprehend-2017-11-27/KeyPhrase)

+ [AWS SDK for Java](http://docs.aws.amazon.com/goto/SdkForJava/comprehend-2017-11-27/KeyPhrase)

+ [AWS SDK for Ruby V2](http://docs.aws.amazon.com/goto/SdkForRubyV2/comprehend-2017-11-27/KeyPhrase)

OutputDataConfig

Provides configuration parameters for the output of topic detection jobs\.

Contents

S3Uri
When you use the `OutputDataConfig` object with the `StartTopicsDetectionJob` operation, you specify the Amazon S3 location where you want to write the output data\. The URI must be in the same region as the API endpoint that you are calling\. The location is used as the prefix for the actual location of the output file\.
When the topic detection job is finished, the service creates an output file in a directory specific to the job\. The `S3Uri` field contains the location of the output file, called `output.tar.gz`\. It is a compressed archive that contains two files, `topic-terms.csv` that lists the terms associated with each topic, and `doc-topics.csv` that lists the documents associated with each topic\. For more information, see [Topic Modeling](topic-modeling.md)\.

Type: String

Length Constraints: Maximum length of 1024\.

444 Pattern: `s3://([^/]+)(/.*)?`
445 Required: Yes
446
447 ## See Also
448
449 For more information about using this API in one of the language\-specific AWS SDKs, see the
       following:
450
451 + [AWS SDK for C\+\+](http://docs.aws.amazon.com/goto/SdkForCpp/comprehend-2017-11-27/
       OutputDataConfig)
452
453 + [AWS SDK for Go](http://docs.aws.amazon.com/goto/SdkForGoV1/comprehend-2017-11-27/
       OutputDataConfig)
454
455 + [AWS SDK for Java](http://docs.aws.amazon.com/goto/SdkForJava/comprehend-2017-11-27/
       OutputDataConfig)
456
457 + [AWS SDK for Ruby V2](http://docs.aws.amazon.com/goto/SdkForRubyV2/comprehend-2017-11-27/
       OutputDataConfig)
458
459
460
461
462 # SentimentScore
463
464 Describes the level of confidence that Amazon Comprehend has in the accuracy of its detection of
       sentiments\.
465
466 ## Contents
467
468 **Mixed**
469 The level of confidence that Amazon Comprehend has in the accuracy of its detection of the `
       MIXED` sentiment\.
470 Type: Float
471 Required: No
472
473 **Negative**
474 The level of confidence that Amazon Comprehend has in the accuracy of its detection of the `
       NEGATIVE` sentiment\.
475 Type: Float
476 Required: No
477
478 **Neutral**
479 The level of confidence that Amazon Comprehend has in the accuracy of its detection of the `
       NEUTRAL` sentiment\.
480 Type: Float
481 Required: No
482
483 **Positive**
484 The level of confidence that Amazon Comprehend has in the accuracy of its detection of the `
       POSITIVE` sentiment\.
485 Type: Float
486 Required: No
487

See Also

For more information about using this API in one of the language\-specific AWS SDKs, see the following:

+ [AWS SDK for C\+\+](http://docs.aws.amazon.com/goto/SdkForCpp/comprehend-2017-11-27/SentimentScore)

+ [AWS SDK for Go](http://docs.aws.amazon.com/goto/SdkForGoV1/comprehend-2017-11-27/SentimentScore)

+ [AWS SDK for Java](http://docs.aws.amazon.com/goto/SdkForJava/comprehend-2017-11-27/SentimentScore)

+ [AWS SDK for Ruby V2](http://docs.aws.amazon.com/goto/SdkForRubyV2/comprehend-2017-11-27/SentimentScore)

TopicsDetectionJobFilter

Provides information for filtering topic detection jobs\. For more information, see [ListTopicsDetectionJobs](API_ListTopicsDetectionJobs.md)\.

Contents

 JobName

Type: String
Length Constraints: Minimum length of 1\. Maximum length of 256\.
Pattern: `^([\p{L}\p{Z}\p{N}_.:/=+\-%@]*)$`
Required: No

 JobStatus
Filters the list of topic detection jobs based on job status\. Returns only jobs with the specified status\.
Type: String
Valid Values:` SUBMITTED | IN_PROGRESS | COMPLETED | FAILED`
Required: No

 SubmitTimeAfter
Filters the list of jobs based on the time that the job was submitted for processing\. Only returns jobs submitted after the specified time\. Jobs are returned in ascending order, oldest to newest\.
Type: Timestamp
Required: No

 SubmitTimeBefore
Filters the list of jobs based on the time that the job was submitted for processing\. Only returns jobs submitted before the specified time\. Jobs are returned in descending order, newest to oldest\.
Type: Timestamp
Required: No

See Also

For more information about using this API in one of the language\-specific AWS SDKs, see the following:

+ [AWS SDK for C\+\+](http://docs.aws.amazon.com/goto/SdkForCpp/comprehend-2017-11-27/TopicsDetectionJobFilter)

+ [AWS SDK for Go](http://docs.aws.amazon.com/goto/SdkForGoV1/comprehend-2017-11-27/TopicsDetectionJobFilter)

+ [AWS SDK for Java](http://docs.aws.amazon.com/goto/SdkForJava/comprehend-2017-11-27/TopicsDetectionJobFilter)

+ [AWS SDK for Ruby V2](http://docs.aws.amazon.com/goto/SdkForRubyV2/comprehend-2017-11-27/TopicsDetectionJobFilter)

TopicsDetectionJobProperties

Provides information about a topic detection job\.

Contents

 EndTime
The time that the topic detection job was completed\.
Type: Timestamp
Required: No

 InputDataConfig
The input data configuration supplied when you created the topic detection job\.
Type: [InputDataConfig](API_InputDataConfig.md) object
Required: No

 JobId
The identifier assigned to the topic detection job\.
Type: String
Length Constraints: Minimum length of 1\. Maximum length of 32\.
Required: No

 JobName
The name of the topic detection job\.
Type: String
Length Constraints: Minimum length of 1\. Maximum length of 256\.
Pattern: `^([\p{L}\p{Z}\p{N}_.:/=+\-%@]*)$`
Required: No

 JobStatus
The current status of the topic detection job\. If the status is `Failed`, the reason for the failure is shown in the `Message` field\.

578 Type: String
579 Valid Values:` SUBMITTED | IN_PROGRESS | COMPLETED | FAILED`
580 Required: No
581
582 **Message**
583 A description for the status of a job\.
584 Type: String
585 Required: No
586
587 **NumberOfTopics**
588 The number of topics to detect supplied when you created the topic detection job\. The default
     is 10\.
589 Type: Integer
590 Required: No
591
592 **OutputDataConfig**   <a name="comprehend-Type-TopicsDetectionJobProperties-OutputDataConfig
     "></a>
593 The output data configuration supplied when you created the topic detection job\.
594 Type: [OutputDataConfig](API_OutputDataConfig.md) object
595 Required: No
596
597 **SubmitTime**
598 The time that the topic detection job was submitted for processing\.
599 Type: Timestamp
600 Required: No
601
602 ## See Also
603
604 For more information about using this API in one of the language\-specific AWS SDKs, see the
     following:
605
606 +   [AWS SDK for C\+\+](http://docs.aws.amazon.com/goto/SdkForCpp/comprehend-2017-11-27/
     TopicsDetectionJobProperties)
607
608 +   [AWS SDK for Go](http://docs.aws.amazon.com/goto/SdkForGoV1/comprehend-2017-11-27/
     TopicsDetectionJobProperties)
609
610 +   [AWS SDK for Java](http://docs.aws.amazon.com/goto/SdkForJava/comprehend-2017-11-27/
     TopicsDetectionJobProperties)
611
612 +   [AWS SDK for Ruby V2](http://docs.aws.amazon.com/goto/SdkForRubyV2/comprehend-2017-11-27/
     TopicsDetectionJobProperties)
613
614
615
616
617 # Common Errors
618
619 This section lists the errors common to the API actions of all AWS services\. For errors
     specific to an API action for this service, see the topic for that API action\.
620
621 **AccessDeniedException**
622 You do not have sufficient access to perform this action\.
623 HTTP Status Code: 400

<pre>
624
625 **IncompleteSignature**
626 The request signature does not conform to AWS standards\.
627 HTTP Status Code: 400
628
629 **InternalFailure**
630 The request processing has failed because of an unknown error, exception or failure\.
631 HTTP Status Code: 500
632
633 **InvalidAction**
634 The action or operation requested is invalid\. Verify that the action is typed correctly\.
635 HTTP Status Code: 400
636
637 **InvalidClientTokenId**
638 The X\.509 certificate or AWS access key ID provided does not exist in our records\.
639 HTTP Status Code: 403
640
641 **InvalidParameterCombination**
642 Parameters that must not be used together were used together\.
643 HTTP Status Code: 400
644
645 **InvalidParameterValue**
646 An invalid or out\-of\-range value was supplied for the input parameter\.
647 HTTP Status Code: 400
648
649 **InvalidQueryParameter**
650 The AWS query string is malformed or does not adhere to AWS standards\.
651 HTTP Status Code: 400
652
653 **MalformedQueryString**
654 The query string contains a syntax error\.
655 HTTP Status Code: 404
656
657 **MissingAction**
658 The request is missing an action or a required parameter\.
659 HTTP Status Code: 400
660
661 **MissingAuthenticationToken**
662 The request must contain either a valid \(registered\) AWS access key ID or X\.509 certificate\.
663 HTTP Status Code: 403
664
665 **MissingParameter**
666 A required parameter for the specified action is not supplied\.
667 HTTP Status Code: 400
668
669 **OptInRequired**
670 The AWS access key ID needs a subscription for the service\.
671 HTTP Status Code: 403
672
673 **RequestExpired**
674 The request reached the service more than 15 minutes after the date stamp on the request or more
        than 15 minutes after the request expiration date \(such as for pre\-signed URLs\), or the
        date stamp on the request is more than 15 minutes in the future\.
675 HTTP Status Code: 400
</pre>

94

676

ServiceUnavailable
The request has failed due to a temporary failure of the server\.
HTTP Status Code: 503

ThrottlingException
The request was denied due to request throttling\.
HTTP Status Code: 400

ValidationError
The input fails to satisfy the constraints specified by an AWS service\.
HTTP Status Code: 400

Common Parameters

The following list contains the parameters that all actions use for signing Signature Version 4 requests with a query string\. Any action\-specific parameters are listed in the topic for that action\. For more information about Signature Version 4, see [Signature Version 4 Signing Process](http://docs.aws.amazon.com/general/latest/gr/signature-version-4.html) in the *Amazon Web Services General Reference*\.

Action
The action to be performed\.
Type: string
Required: Yes

Version
The API version that the request is written for, expressed in the format YYYY\-MM\-DD\.
Type: string
Required: Yes

X\-Amz\-Algorithm
The hash algorithm that you used to create the request signature\.
Condition: Specify this parameter when you include authentication information in a query string instead of in the HTTP authorization header\.
Type: string
Valid Values: `AWS4-HMAC-SHA256`
Required: Conditional

X\-Amz\-Credential
The credential scope value, which is a string that includes your access key, the date, the region you are targeting, the service you are requesting, and a termination string \("aws4_request"\)\. The value is expressed in the following format: *access_key*/*YYYYMMDD*/*region*/*service*/aws4_request\.
For more information, see [Task 2: Create a String to Sign for Signature Version 4](http://docs.aws.amazon.com/general/latest/gr/sigv4-create-string-to-sign.html) in the *Amazon Web Services General Reference*\.
Condition: Specify this parameter when you include authentication information in a query string instead of in the HTTP authorization header\.
Type: string
Required: Conditional

719

720 **X\-Amz\-Date**

721 The date that is used to create the signature\. The format must be ISO 8601 basic format \(
    YYYYMMDD'T'HHMMSS'Z'\)\. For example, the following date time is a valid X\-Amz\-Date value:
    `20120325T120000Z`\.

722 Condition: X\-Amz\-Date is optional for all requests; it can be used to override the date used
    for signing requests\. If the Date header is specified in the ISO 8601 basic format, X\-Amz
    \-Date is not required\. When X\-Amz\-Date is used, it always overrides the value of the
    Date header\. For more information, see [Handling Dates in Signature Version 4](http://docs.
    aws.amazon.com/general/latest/gr/sigv4-date-handling.html) in the *Amazon Web Services
    General Reference*\.

723 Type: string

724 Required: Conditional

725

726 **X\-Amz\-Security\-Token**

727 The temporary security token that was obtained through a call to AWS Security Token Service \(
    AWS STS\)\. For a list of services that support temporary security credentials from AWS
    Security Token Service, go to [AWS Services That Work with IAM](http://docs.aws.amazon.com/
    IAM/latest/UserGuide/reference_aws-services-that-work-with-iam.html) in the *IAM User Guide
    *\.

728 Condition: If you're using temporary security credentials from the AWS Security Token Service,
    you must include the security token\.

729 Type: string

730 Required: Conditional

731

732 **X\-Amz\-Signature**

733 Specifies the hex\-encoded signature that was calculated from the string to sign and the derived
    signing key\.

734 Condition: Specify this parameter when you include authentication information in a query string
    instead of in the HTTP authorization header\.

735 Type: string

736 Required: Conditional

737

738 **X\-Amz\-SignedHeaders**

739 Specifies all the HTTP headers that were included as part of the canonical request\. For more
    information about specifying signed headers, see [Task 1: Create a Canonical Request For
    Signature Version 4](http://docs.aws.amazon.com/general/latest/gr/sigv4-create-canonical-
    request.html) in the * Amazon Web Services General Reference*\.

740 Condition: Specify this parameter when you include authentication information in a query string
    instead of in the HTTP authorization header\.

741 Type: string

742 Required: Conditional

743

744

745

746

747 # Document History for Amazon Comprehend

748

749 The following table describes the documentation for this release of Amazon Comprehend\.

750

751 + **Latest documentation update:**November 29, 2017

752

753

754 ****

Change	Description	Date
New guide	This is the first release of the Amazon Comprehend Developer Guide\.	November 29, 2017

www.ingramcontent.com/pod-product-compliance
Lightning Source LLC
LaVergne TN
LVHW082040050326
832904LV00005B/255